A LIVING REALITY

A LIVING REALITY

The Faith Principle
in the Life of George Müller

Roger Steer

HODDER AND STOUGHTON
LONDON SYDNEY AUCKLAND TORONTO
AND
STL BOOKS, BROMLEY, KENT

STL BOOKS are published by
Send The Light (Operation Mobilisation),
PO BOX 48, Bromley, Kent, England.

British Library Cataloguing in Publication Data

Steer, Roger
  A living reality.
  1. Muller, George, 1805-1898   2. Christian
  biography———England———Bristol   3. Bristol
  (Avon)———Orphanages———History
  I. Title
  362.7'32'0924   HV28.M77

HODDER & STOUGHTON
ISBN 0 340 37207 9

STL
ISBN 0 903843 96 X

*Hodder and Stoughton Editorial Office: 47 Bedford Square, London WC1B
3DP*

Contents

Prologue

Prologue

The story of George Müller's life is one of the most remarkable episodes in the history of the Christian Church.

Müller set out to demonstrate that, as he put it, there is 'reality in the things of God'. He took a bold view of Christianity. For him Christianity was more than a fine system of ethics, the account of a people who believed in a Creator God and the story of the life, death and resurrection of Jesus, though he believed it was all these things. For him Christianity concerned a God who remained in the nineteenth century a living reality, who knew and loved George Müller and who intervened in the affairs of men and women in answer to prayer. Müller put this belief to the test for over seventy years, after becoming a Christian at the age of twenty.

He embarked on the venture of faith which was to make him famous just as Charles Dickens was writing *Oliver Twist* – the novel which drew the public's attention to one of Britain's major social problems, the plight of orphans.

The reasons which led Müller to embark on his project are set out in part one. Müller summarised the challenge which faced him like this:

Now if I, a poor man, simply by prayer and faith, obtained, *without asking any individual*, the means for establishing and carrying on an orphan-house: there would be something which, with the Lord's blessing, might be instrumental in strengthening the faith of the children of God, besides being a testimony to the consciences of the unconverted of the reality of the things of God.

Müller opened his first children's home in April 1836 at the age of thirty. Though he went quietly about his work, his little home in Bristol for thirty children amounted to an invitation to unbelievers to watch the work he had begun to see if there was a God who would finance it. And here was a challenge to believers not only to see what God would do, but to consider their response if He proved faithful.

What happened? During the next sixty-three years Müller received nearly one and a half million pounds; and the many branches of his work included the care of some ten thousand children. He claimed that neither he nor his staff ever issued an appeal for funds or asked any individual to support his work. No evidence has been produced to disprove this. It was once alleged that Müller had prayed publicly that God would send money to his homes. When this allegation was drawn to his attention, Müller (and no one ever doubted his transparent honesty) described it as 'entirely false'. He commented that, 'So far from wishing to make known our need for the purpose of influencing benevolent persons to contribute the necessities of the institution under my care, I have even refused to let our circumstances be known, after having been asked about them, when on simply saying that we were in need I might have had considerable sums.'

I told the story of Müller's life in *George Müller: Delighted in God**. My objective in this book is different. I have concentrated on Müller's experience of God and, using a good deal of source material which was inappropriate for a biography, have in the main allowed Müller to speak for himself. I have arranged the extracts from his writings and sermons thematically rather than in strict chronological order, but in the linking passages I have tried to give enough information about Müller's life and achievements to enable you to understand the quotations selected. At the end of the book I have listed the main events of Müller's life. The divisions between the six parts are somewhat arbitrary, and there is a good deal of overlap. Despite the heading of part six, there are passages of personal application throughout the book.

After his conversion, Müller became (not quite all at once) a man of great integrity, utterly committed to serving God. Rarely in his writings does he attack anything. He was *for* God, *for* happiness, *for* goodness, *for* that which is

* Hodder Christian Paperback, 1981.

wholesome. There is nothing negative, never a hint of cynicism. There is a freshness and vitality in his style, but nowhere a striving for novel or *outré* themes. By the end of his life, he had read through the Bible over one hundred times and his attitude towards it was one of total humility and obedience.

I hope that this book will throw light on a number of questions, namely:

What is faith? A brave belief in that which is inherently improbable? A commitment to certainties? An excuse for *doing* nothing? A special gift of God not available to all?

Can faith grow and, if so, how? What is the relationship between faith and sight, and between faith and presumption? Docs faith work? Müller both exercised faith and reflected on its nature. Parts two and six set out his conclusions.

What is prayer? A healthy attitude of mind in which we acknowledge our dependence on someone greater than ourselves? An opportunity to express our selfless concern for others? The process by which we get to know God's will for our lives?

Müller agreed that it was all this. But there was much more as parts three and six will show.

How important is the Bible, nearly two thousand years after its most recent parts were written? How should we read it to gain the maximum benefit, and what is the relationship between Bible study and prayer? Part four gives Müller's distinctive answers.

What about fund raising? In the last quarter of the twentieth century many forms of Christian enterprise are expensive. Missionary societies, coordinators of evangelical crusades, local churches planning extensions to their premises or struggling to maintain them, organisers of community outreach are all faced with the need to raise large sums of money. The debate as to how this should be done is often an interesting one. Reservations may be expressed about the techniques used: elaborate appeals for funds (or more subtle hints), sponsored walks, jumble sales, stewardship campaigns, carefully directed letters to the administrators of trust funds and so on. The names of giants of faith like Müller are sometimes injected into the discussion. Did he not raise large sums of money simply through prayer and faith? Has God changed? The pages which follow show that Müller does indeed have a contribution to make to this debate by inspiring individual believers to deepen their commitment to Christ and to trust God more completely in all areas of their Christian service, and by clarifying which aspects of his life's work were something personal – a feature of his unique attempt to demonstrate God's reality – and those which were of universal application.

Some key passages which encapsulate Müller's views on fund raising are on pages 45–49 and 110–113, but you will not grasp their full significance until you begin to appreciate Müller's experience of God in every area of his life.

Finally Müller has an answer to the most fundamental of questions – *Is there a God?*

Müller lived at a time when the historic Christian faith was under attack: first from those who drew atheistic conclusions from the theory of evolution; then from the development of social theories, including those of Marx, Bentham and Mill, which left little room for Christianity; and finally from a school of Biblical criticism (based in Müller's homeland) which sought to destroy the supernatural nature of the Bible, seeing it as the record of the growth of religious ideas in human consciousness.

It was against this background that Arthur Tappan Pierson recorded that many readers of George Müller's *Narratives* found them 'the most wonderful and complete refutation of scepticism it had ever been their lot to meet with'. W. H. Harding said that the 'story of George Müller's life presents one of the most striking testimonies to the faithfulness of God that the world has ever seen'. In 1879 a house agent wrote to Müller and told him that reading the story of his life had totally changed his own inner life to one of perfect trust and confidence in God. The letter was typical of many Müller received. My prayer is that you will find this new collection of Müller's writings and addresses similarly inspiring.

1

The Visible Proof

Why Müller acted as he did

The reality of the things of God

In 1832, at the age of twenty-six, Müller became pastor of Bethesda chapel in Bristol, and four years later he opened his first children's home. In 1837, in *Oliver Twist*, Charles Dickens drew the British public's attention to the desperate plight of orphan children, and in the early summer of the same year, while confined to his home with a foot injury, Müller wrote the first part of his *Narratives of some of the Lord's dealings with George Müller*. In this extract he sets out the reasons why he had embarked on his venture of faith.

Through my pastoral labours among the saints in Bristol, through my considerable correspondence, and through brethren who visited Bristol, I had constantly cases brought before me which proved that one of the especial things which the children of God needed in our day was *to have their faith strengthened*.

For instance: I might visit a brother who worked fourteen or even sixteen hours a day at his trade, the necessary result of which was that not only his body suffered, but his soul was lean, and he had no enjoyment of the things of God. Under such circumstances I might point out to him that he ought to work less, in order that his bodily health might not suffer, and that he might gather strength for his inner man by reading the Word of God, by meditation over it, and by prayer.

The reply, however, I generally found to be something like this: 'But if I work less, I do not earn enough for the support of my family. Even now, whilst I work so much, I have scarcely enough. The wages are so low that I must work hard in order to obtain what I need.'

There was no trust in God. No real belief in the truth of that word: 'Seek first the kingdom of God, and His righteousness: and all these things shall be added unto you.'

I might reply something like this: 'My dear brother, it is not your work which supports your family, but the Lord; and

He who has fed you and your family when you could not work at all, on account of illness, would surely provide for you and yours, if, for the sake of obtaining food for your inner man, you were to work only for so many hours a day as would allow you proper time for retirement. And is it not the case now that you begin the work of the day after having had only a few hurried moments for prayer; and when you leave off your work in the evening, and mean to read a little of the Word of God, are you not too worn out in body and mind to enjoy it, and do you not often fall asleep whilst reading the Scriptures, or whilst on your knees in prayer?'

The brother would allow that it was so; he would allow that my advice was good; but still I read in his countenance, even if he should not have actually said so, 'How should I get on, if I were to *carry out* your advice?'

I longed therefore to have something to point the brother to, as a visible proof that our God and Father is the same faithful God as ever He was; as willing as ever to prove Himself to be the living God in our day as formerly to all who put their trust in Him...

Another class of persons were brethren in business who suffered in their souls, and brought guilt on their consciences, by carrying on their business almost in the same way as unconverted persons do. The competition in trade, the bad times, the over-peopled country were given as reasons why, if the business were carried on simply according to the Word of God, it could not be expected to do well. Such a brother, perhaps, would express the wish that he might be differently situated; but very rarely did I see that there was a stand made for God, that there was the holy determination to trust in the living God, and to depend on Him, in order that a good conscience might be maintained. To this class likewise I desired to show, by a visible proof, that God is unchangeably the same...

My spirit longed to be instrumental in strengthening their faith by giving them not only instances from the Word of God of His willingness and ability to help all those who rely upon Him, but to show them by proofs that He is the same in our day. I well knew that the Word of God ought to be enough, and it was by grace enough to me; but still I considered that I ought to lend a helping hand to my brethren, if by any means, by this visible proof to the unchangeable faithfulness of the Lord, I might strengthen their hands in God; for I remembered what a great blessing my own soul had received through the Lord's dealings with his servant A. H. Franke, who, in dependence upon the living God alone, established an immense orphan-house which I had seen many times with my own eyes. [August Franke (1663–1727) established free schools and an orphan house in Halle in the closing years of the seventeenth century.]

I therefore judged myself bound to be the servant of the Church of Christ in the particular point on which I had obtained mercy: namely, *in being able to take God by His Word and to rely upon it.* All these exercises of my soul, which resulted from the fact that so many believers with whom I became acquainted were harassed and distressed in mind, or brought guilt on their consciences, on account of not trusting in the Lord, were used by God to awaken in my heart the desire of setting before the Church at large, and before the world, a proof that He has not in the least changed; and this seemed to me best done by the establishing of an orphan-house. It needed to be something which could be seen even by the natural eye.

Now if I, a poor man, simply by prayer and faith, obtained, *without asking any individual*, the means for establishing and carrying on an orphan-house, there would be something which, with the Lord's blessing, might be instrumental in strengthening the faith of the children of God, besides being a testimony to the consciences of the unconverted of the reality of the things of God.

This, then, was the primary reason for establishing the orphan-house. I certainly did from my heart desire to be used by God to benefit the bodies of poor children, bereaved of both parents, and seek, in other respects, with the help of God, to do them good for this life; I also particularly longed to be used by God in getting the dear orphans trained up in the fear of God; but still, the first and primary object of the work was (and still is): that God might be magnified by the fact that the orphans under my care are provided with all they need only *by prayer and faith*, without anyone being asked by me or my fellow-labourers, whereby it may be seen that God is *faithful still*, and *hears prayer still*.

Nearly forty years later, in 1874 (when he still had nearly a quarter of a century to live), Müller wrote:

I have joyfully dedicated my life to this great end, to give a practical demonstration to all who need it of the blessedness and power of the life of faith.

2

Stayed upon God

*A look at Müller's life
of faith*

The loveliness of God

Müller's faith sprang from his delight in God. Throughout his life, God was – for Müller – not a vague impersonal force but a living reality, a friend every moment of the day. He told the congregation at Salem Chapel, Bristol, in July 1871, that:

No one ever knew Jehovah without being able to exercise faith in Him. It is when God is not known that difficulty comes. The great point therefore is to acquaint ourselves with God, to know God for ourselves as He has revealed Himself in the Scriptures.

And addressing one of the Clifton Conferences of Christians he took up the theme of zeal for God.

This zeal for God allows of an increase or a decrease *in ourselves*; and it will be found to increase in the measure in which our hearts are practically entering into the loveliness of the nature and character of God. We have therefore to seek for ourselves to become more and more convinced of the graciousness of God, of His love, His bountifulness, His kindness, His pity, His compassion, His readiness to help and bless, His patience, His faithfulness, His almighty power, His infinite wisdom; in a word, we have to seek to know God, not according to the views of men, not even according to the notions of Christians generally, but according to the revelation He has made of Himself in the Holy Scriptures.

Why is it important to know more of God? Müller answered the question at a United Meeting for Prayer held in the Broadmead Rooms, Bristol, in January, 1870.

Because it tends to holiness, happiness, and usefulness. It tends to holiness: the more I know of God, the more I am constrained to admire Him, and to say, 'What a lovely, good being He is!' And especially when I see His wondrous love in Christ Jesus to such a guilty, wicked creature as I am; and therefore my heart is constrained to seek to imitate God, to seek to do something in return for His love, and to be more like God Himself.

It also tends to happiness: the more we know of God, the happier we are. It was when we were in entire ignorance of God that we were without real peace or joy. When we became a little acquainted with God, our peace and joy – our true happiness, I mean – commenced; and the more we become acquainted with Him, the more truly happy we become. What will make us so exceedingly happy in Heaven? It will be the fuller knowledge of God – we shall know Him far better than we now do.

The knowledge of God also tends to our usefulness in His service here: it is impossible that I can enter into what God has done for sinners, without being constrained in return to seek to live for Him, to labour for Him. I ask myself, 'What can I do for Him who has bestowed upon me His choicest gifts?' Hence I am constrained to labour for Him. According to the measure in which I am fully acquainted with God, do I seek to labour for Him. I cannot be idle.

The promises of God's Word

Müller grew up and was educated in Germany (then the kingdom of Prussia). He came to England in March, 1829, at the age of twenty-three. Originally he had intended to work with the London Society for Promoting Christianity Amongst the Jews, but for a number of reasons became disenchanted and – after some months deliberation and prayer – decided to end his link with the Society.

One of the issues he had to consider in making his decision to break with the Society was how his financial needs were to be met. In his *Narratives* he described how he resolved this:

There remained now only one point more to be settled: how I should do for the future as it regarded the supply of my temporal wants, which naturally would have been a great obstacle especially as I was not merely a foreigner, but spoke so little English that, whilst I was greatly assisted in expounding the Scriptures, it was with difficulty I could converse about common things. On this point, however, I had no anxiety; for I considered that as long as I really sought to serve the Lord, that is as long as I sought the kingdom of God and His righteousness, these my temporal supplies would be added to me. The Lord mercifully enabled me to take the promises of His Word and rest upon them, and such as Matthew 7:7–8, John 14:13–14 and Matthew 6:25–34 were the stay of my soul concerning this point.

These passages, which are all the words of Jesus, are (in the New International Version of the Bible):

Matthew 7:7–8: 'Ask and it will be given to you; seek and you will find; knock and the door will be opened to you. For everyone who asks receives; he who seeks finds; and to him who knocks, the door will be opened.'

John 14:13–14: 'And I will do whatever you ask in My name, so that the Son may bring glory to the Father. You may ask Me for anything in My name, and I will do it.'

Matthew 6:25–34: 'Therefore I tell you, do not worry about your life, what you will eat or drink; or about your body, what you will wear. Is not life more important than food, and the body more important than clothes? Look at the birds of the air; they do not sow or reap or store away in barns, and yet your Heavenly Father feeds them. Are you not much more valuable than they? Who of you by worrying can add a single hour to his life?

'And why do you worry about clothes? See how the lilies of the field grow. They do not labour or spin. Yet I tell you that not even Solomon in all his splendour was dressed like one of these. If that is how God clothes the grass of the field, which is here today and tomorrow is thrown into the fire, will He not much more clothe you, O you of little faith? So do not worry, saying, "What shall we eat?" or "What shall we drink?" or "What shall we wear?" For the pagans run after all these things, and your Heavenly Father knows that you need them. But seek first His kingdom and His righteousness, and all these things will be given to you as well. Therefore do not worry about tomorrow, for tomorrow will worry about itself.

Each day has enough trouble of its own.'

Müller took Jesus at His word. What was the result? In 1864 he recorded in his journal:

It is now about forty-four years since I have had any regular income whatever. In the year 1830, I saw it to be the Lord's will to give up my regular income in connexion with the ministry of the Word, and to trust in Him alone for the supply of all my temporal necessities. I have been enabled to continue in this path, and have not been allowed to regret the step which I then took.

Thus it is also in my position as director of the various objects of the Scriptural Knowledge Institution [see page 27 below]. I have no salary in this position; but the Lord abundantly supplies my need; indeed, though there are many expenses connected with this very position, He abundantly meets all my wants, and gives me far more than I need. If I had earnestly sought to obtain a lucrative place, either as a preacher of the Gospel, or in some other way, I should not have had nearly as much, I have reason to believe, as, unsought, unasked for (so far as it regards man), I receive day by day out of the loving hand of my Heavenly Father.

When I look at His kindness to me in saving my guilty soul, I am overwhelmed with the boundlessness of His love and grace towards me in Christ Jesus; and when I look at His kindness to me, even as it regards temporal things, I know not where to begin, nor where to end, in speaking well of His name.

Details of the money Müller received for his personal expenses and of his giving during his life-time are given on page 107.

Freedom from anxiety

Müller denied that living without a salary made him anxious. In the first part of his *Narratives* he wrote:

If any of the children of God should think that such a mode of living leads away from the Lord, and from caring about spiritual things, and has the effect of causing the mind to be taken up with the question, What shall I eat? What shall I drink? And Wherewithal shall I be clothed? And that on that account it would be much better to have a stated salary, particularly for one who labours in the Word and doctrine, in order that he may be above these cares; I say, should any believer think so, I would request him prayerfully to consider the following remarks.

1. I have had experience of both ways, and know that my present mode of living, as to temporal things, is connected with less care.

2. Confidence in the Lord, to whom alone I look for the supply of my temporal wants, keeps me, at least while faith is in exercise, when a case of distress comes before me, or when the Lord's work calls for my pecuniary aid, from anxious reckoning like this: Will my salary last out? Shall I have enough myself the next month? In this my freedom, I am, by the grace of God, generally at least able to say to myself something like this: my Lord is not limited; He can again supply; He knows that this present case has been sent to me; and thus this way of living, so far from *leading to anxiety*, as it regards possible future want, is rather the means of *keeping from it*. And truly it was once said to me by an individual, ' You can do such and such things, and need not to lay by, for the Church in the whole of Devonshire cares about your wants.' My reply was: the Lord can use not merely any of the saints throughout Devonshire, but those throughout the world as instruments to supply my temporal wants.

3. This way of living has often been the means of reviving the work of grace in my heart when I have been getting cold; and it has also been the means of bringing me back to the Lord after I have been backsliding. For it will not do – it is not possible – to live in sin, and, at the same time, by communion with God, to draw down from Heaven everything one needs for the life that now is.

4. Frequently, too, a fresh answer to prayer obtained in this way has been the means of quickening my soul, and filling me with much joy.

In 1874, after forty years as Director of the Scriptural

Knowledge Institution, Müller wrote:

I cannot tell you how happy this service makes me. Instead of being the anxious, careworn man many persons think me to be, I have no anxieties and no cares at all. Faith in God leads me to roll *all* my burdens upon Him.

Müller's longevity (he died when he was ninety-two) surely confirms his insistence that he was not worn out by worry. And a west-country farmer said (when Müller was sixty), 'I was going up Ashley Hill the other morning when I met Mr Müller walking towards the city. Had I not known him, I should have said that he was a gentleman of leisure and without a care, so quietly did he walk and so peaceful and stately was his demeanour! The twenty-third Psalm seemed written on his face.'

Joy in the Holy Spirit

Freedom from anxiety is one thing; joy is something even more positive. In his journal for September 8, 1838, Müller recorded:

Yesterday and today I have been pleading with God eleven arguments why He would be graciously pleased to send help. My mind has been at peace respecting the matter. Yesterday the peace amounted even to joy in the Holy Spirit.

Nearly forty years later, on a Sunday morning in August, 1876, Müller told a large congregation at the Tabernacle, Penn Street, Bristol:

I am happier now, after being a believer nearly fifty-one years, than I was fifty years ago; happier far than I was forty years ago, than I was thirty years ago, than I was twenty years ago, than I was ten years ago. As the time has gone on, my peace and joy and happiness in the Lord have increased more and more, instead of going more and more.

Why do I refer to this? Not to boast, for it is all by the grace of God; but to encourage my younger fellow-believers to expect greater things from the Lord, who delights in giving abundantly. And as you sing sometimes, 'More and more, more and more,' there is yet more to come. Let us look out for it, for God delights to give more grace. It is the joy and delight of His heart to give more and more.

Why should it not be? Why should we not in the last part of life have the best things? Has God changed? Far from it! Is the Bible changed? No! We have the same blessed Word. Is the power of the Holy Spirit less? Far different from that; nothing of the kind! The Lord Jesus Christ is ever ready to bless. The Word we now have is the whole revelation. And our Heavenly Father has the same heart toward His children. Therefore there is nothing to hinder our being happier as time goes with us.

A big faith

Müller's faith was by no means just for money. In 1845 he wrote:

By the grace of God I desire that my faith in God should extend towards EVERY thing, the smallest of my own temporal and spiritual concerns, and the smallest of the temporal and spiritual concerns of my family, towards the saints among whom I labour, the Church at large, everything that has to do with the temporal and spiritual prosperity of the Scriptural Knowledge Institution.

The Scriptural Knowledge Institution was the name Müller had given to the body he had founded in 1834. Its interests were far wider than the residential care of children, and during his life the Institution laid out nearly half a million pounds on objects other than the orphan work. Of this nearly a hundred and fifteen thousand pounds was spent on day-schools throughout the world. The Institution entirely financed nearly eighty day-schools for children and half a dozen adult schools, so that in the years 1879–80 Müller was responsible for the education of over seven thousand children. Of these schools, there were fourteen in Spain, four in India, one in Italy, six in British Guiana and over fifty in England and Wales. In the same year he entirely financed nearly forty Sunday schools and assisted a further fourteen.

The Institution spent nearly ninety thousand pounds on the circulation of Bibles, testaments, tracts and books and over two hundred and sixty thousand pounds on world-wide missionary work. In the peak years of the missionary work in the early 1870s, Müller sent ten thousand pounds abroad annually to nearly two hundred missionaries – including, notably, Hudson Taylor and the founders of the China Inland Mission. All this was in addition to the care and education of two thousand children in his five houses on Ashley Down.

But the need for finance was simply one of many concerns, as Müller explained in 1875:

The pecuniary necessities for which we have to wait upon the Lord, great though they are, amounting to about forty-four thousand pounds yearly, are very far from all we need. We have constantly to look to the Lord for counsel and guidance in our difficulties; and but for His constant guidance, we should make only mistakes and take wrong steps.

We have further continually almost to ask the Lord for the needed helpers either for the orphan houses or the very many schools, or other branches of the Institution. And this is not a little matter, to obtain not only truly godly helpers, but at the same time persons who in other respects also are fitted for such service.

Further, we have to wait upon the Lord not a little to know how, in certain circumstances, to deal with regard to the children; for it is not of rare occurrence that our circumstances in this respect are of a most perplexing character.

Further, the orphans are to be placed out, whether the boys as indoor apprentices, or the girls to be sent to service. Here we are entirely thrown upon God to find masters and mistresses who not only are Christians indeed, and not in name only, but who also in other respects, as far as we are able to judge, are suitable to have the care of these orphans when they leave us.

Then we have the difficulty of grave illness on the part of

the helpers in the work or the children under our care, and this sometimes of a very alarming character in such epidemics as scarlet fever, small pox, etc. But God, to whom we seek to look continually for help, at all times and under all circumstances helps us, and we have never been confounded. A number of other things might be referred to, to show that money is not the only thing which we need, and for which we trust in the Lord.

Faith for healing

Soon after arriving in England in 1829, Müller became quite seriously ill. He had been far from well in Germany and had been rejected from army service on health grounds. In London he felt sure he was dying, but after a fortnight's illness his doctor told him that he would recover and he was advised to go to Devon to convalesce. The sea-air at Teignmouth did the trick and it was as a result of contacts made there that he became pastor of a small chapel in the town. His journal for February, 1832, contains some remarkable entries and also indicates that the recovery was not yet quite complete. Müller was twenty-six at this time.

February 18. This afternoon I broke a blood vessel in my stomach, and lost a considerable quantity of blood. I was very happy immediately afterwards.

February 19. This morning, Lord's day, two brethren [from the chapel] called on me to ask what arrangement there should be made today as it regarded the four villages where some of the brethren were in the habit of preaching, as, on account of my not being able to preach, one of the brethren would need to stay at home to take my place. I asked them kindly to come again in about an hour when I would give them an answer.

After they had gone, the Lord gave me faith to rise. I dressed myself, and determined to go to the chapel. I was enabled to do so, though so weak when I went that walking the short distance to the chapel was an exertion to me. I was enabled to preach this morning with as loud and strong a voice as usual, and for the usual length of time.

After the morning meeting, a medical friend called on me and entreated me not to preach again in the afternoon as it might greatly injure me. I told him that I should indeed consider it great presumption to do so had the Lord not given me faith. I preached again in the afternoon and this medical friend called again and said the same concerning the evening meeting. Nevertheless, having faith, I preached again in the evening.

After each meeting I became stronger, which was a plain proof that the hand of God was in the matter. After the third meeting I went immediately to bed, considering that it would be presumption to try my strength needlessly.

February 20. The Lord enabled me to rise early in the morning, and to go to our usual Prayer-meeting where I read, spoke and prayed. Afterwards I wrote four letters, expounded the Scriptures at home, and attended the meeting again in the evening.

February 21. I attended the two meetings as usual, preached in the evening, and did my other work besides.

February 22. Today I attended the meeting in the morning, walked afterwards six miles with two brethren to Newton Bushel, and rode from thence to Plymouth.

February 23. I am now as well as I was before I broke the blood vessel.

In his *Narratives* Müller commented on these entries in his journal.

I would earnestly warn everyone who may read this not to imitate me in such a thing if he has no faith; but if he has, it will, as a good coin, most assuredly be honoured by God. I could not say that if such a thing should happen again I would act in the same way; for when I have been not nearly so weak as when I had broken the blood vessel, having no faith, I did not preach; yet if it were to please the Lord to give me faith I might be able to do the same, though even weaker than at the time just spoken of.

About this time I repeatedly prayed with sick believers until they were restored. *Unconditionally* I asked the Lord for the blessing of bodily health (a thing which I could not do now), and almost always had the petition answered. In some instances, however, the prayer was not answered. In the same way, whilst in London in November, 1829, in answer to my prayers, I was immediately restored from a bodily infirmity under which I had been labouring for a long time and which has never returned since.

The way in which I now account for these facts is as follows. It pleased the Lord, I think, to give me in such cases something like the gift (not the grace) of faith, so that unconditionally I could ask and look for the answer. The difference between the *gift* and the *grace* of faith seems to me this:

According to the *gift of faith* I am able to do a thing, or believe that a thing will come to pass, the not doing of which, or the not believing of which, *would not be a sin*; according to *the grace of faith* I am able to do a thing, or believe that a thing will come to pass, respecting which I have the Word of God as the ground to rest upon, and therefore the not doing it, or the not believing it, *would be sin*. For instance, *the gift of faith* would be needed to believe that a sick person should be restored again, though there is no human probability: for *there is no promise to that effect*; *the grace of faith* is needed to believe that the Lord will give me the necessaries of life, if I first seek the kingdom of God and His righteousness: for *there is a promise to that effect* in Matthew 6.

The gift of faith

Later in his life, in 1869, Müller expanded on this theme of the gift of faith.

Think not that I have *the gift of faith* of which we read in 1 Corinthians 12:9 for the following reasons:

1. The faith which I am enabled to exercise with reference to the orphan-houses and my own temporal necessities is not that faith of which it is said in 1 Corinthians 13:2 (evidently in allusion to the faith spoken in 1 Corinthians 12:9), 'If I have a faith that can move mountains, but have not love, I am nothing'; it is the self-same faith which is found in *every*

believer, and the growth of which I am most sensible of to myself; for, little by little, it has been increasing for the last forty-three years.

2. This faith which is exercised respecting the orphan-houses and my own temporal necessities shows itself in the same measure, for instance, concerning the following points: I have never been permitted to doubt during the last forty-three years that my sins are forgiven, that I am a child of God, that I am beloved of God, and that I shall be finally saved; because I am enabled, by the grace of God, to exercise faith upon the Word of God, and believe what God says in those passages which settle these matters (1 John 5:1; Galatians 3:26; Acts 10:43; Romans 10:9–10; John 3:16 etc.).

Further, at the time when I thought I should be insane [in 1837–38 Müller was unwell for seven months with a nervous illness and feared insanity], I was in peace, quite in peace, because my soul believed the truth of that word, 'We know that all things work together for good to them that love God' (Rom. 8: 28).

Further, when my brother and my dear aged father died, and when concerning both of them I had no *evidence* whatever that they were saved (though I dare not say that they are lost, for I know it not); yet my soul was at peace, perfectly at peace, under this great trial, this exceedingly great trial. And what was it that gave me peace? My soul laid hold on that word, 'Shall not the judge of all the world do right?' This word, together with the character of God, as He revealed Himself in His holy Word, settled all questionings. I believed what He has said concerning Himself, and I was at peace, and have been at peace ever since, concerning this matter.

Further, when the Lord took from me a beloved infant [in 1835 the Müllers' son Elijah died of pneumonia, aged fifteen months] my soul was at peace, perfectly at peace; I could only weep tears of joy when I did weep. And why? Because my soul laid hold in faith on that word, 'Of such is the kingdom of Heaven' (Matt. 19:14). Believing therefore as I did upon the ground of this word, my soul rejoiced, instead of mourning, that my beloved infant was far happier with the Lord than with me.

Further, when sometimes all has been dark, exceedingly dark, with reference to my service among the saints, judging from natural appearances; yea, when I should have been overwhelmed indeed in grief and despair, had I looked at things after the outward appearance: at such times I have sought to encourage myself in God, by laying hold in faith on His mighty power, His unchangeable love, and His infinite wisdom, and I have said to myself: God is able and willing to deliver me, if it be good for me; for it is written: 'He that spared not His own Son, but delivered Him up for us all, how shall He not with Him also freely give us all things?' (Rom. 8:32) This it was which, being believed by me through grace, kept my soul in peace.

Further, when in connexion with the orphan-houses, day-schools, etc., trials have come upon me which were far heavier than the want of means, when lying reports were spread that the orphans had not enough to eat, or that they were cruelly treated in other respects, and the like; or when other trials still greater, but which I cannot mention, have befallen me in connexion with this work, and that at a time when I was nearly a thousand miles absent from Bristol, and had to remain absent week after week: at such times my soul was stayed upon God; I believed His word of promise which was applicable to such cases; I poured out my soul before God, and arose from my knees in peace, because the trouble that was in the soul was in believing prayer cast upon God, and thus I was kept in peace, though I saw it to be the will of God to remain far away from the work.

Dear reader, I may seem to boast; but, by the grace of God, I do not boast in thus speaking. From my inmost soul I do ascribe it to God alone that He enabled me to trust in Him, and that hitherto He has not suffered my confidence in Him to fail. But I thought it needful to make these remarks, lest anyone should think that my depending upon God was a particular gift given to me, which other saints have no right to look for; or lest it should be thought that this my depending upon Him had only to do with the obtaining of money by prayer and faith.

Do not think that I have attained in faith (and how much less in other respects!) to that degree to which I might and ought to attain; but thank God for the faith which He has given me, and ask Him to uphold and increase it.

Faith and sight

The winter of 1846–7 was not an easy time for meeting the day-to-day needs of the children in Müller's care. 1846 was a year of catastrophic crop failure both of wheat and potatoes, prices soared and in May, 1847, Müller recorded:

Never were provisions nearly so dear since the commencement of the work as they are now. Bread is almost twice as much as eighteen months ago, oatmeal nearly three times as much as formerly, rice more than double the usual price, and no potatoes can be used on account of their exceedingly high price.

But, he added:

The children have lacked nothing.

And commented:

I remember to have heard the following remarks with reference to the season of dearth during the winter of 1846–7: 'I wonder how it is now with the orphans? If Mr Müller is now able to provide for them as he has, we will say nothing.' When I heard such remarks, I said nothing except: 'We lack nothing,' or 'God helps us.'

Should this fall into the hands of any who have had such thoughts, let them remember that it is the very time for *faith* to work, when *sight* ceases. The greater the difficulties, the easier for faith. As long as there remain certain natural prospects, faith does not get on as easily (if I may say so), as when all natural prospects fail.

It is true that during the time of dearth our expenses were considerably greater than usual; it is also true that many persons who otherwise might have given were unable to do so, or had their surplus directed into other channels such as Ireland; but the gold and silver are the Lord's. To Him we made our prayer. In Him we put our trust. And He did not forsake us. For we went as easily through the winter as through any winter since the work had been in existence. Nor could it be otherwise; for God had at this very time an especial opportunity of showing the blessedness of trusting in Him.

Müller concluded an address at one of the Clifton Conferences of Christians, at which he had taken as his text 2 Corinthians 5:7, 'We walk by faith, not by sight,' with these words:

We have to believe what God says. Nor must we look to our feelings, nor expect help from our natural fallen reason; nor must we be discouraged though all appearance were against what God says; for faith begins when sight fails. As long as we can see with the natural eye, and our natural fallen reason will yet help us, faith is not needed.

This is often lost sight of by the children of God; and hence they are so much discouraged because they do not walk by sight which was never intended for them while they are still in the body. If there is one thing that we need more than another it is an increase of faith in order that we may take right steps, surer steps, firmer steps; yea, run with alacrity in the ways of the Lord. To the end of our course we therefore should pray, 'Lord, increase my faith!'

Faith and the presence of God

In 1841, Müller wrote:

This way of living brings the Lord remarkably near. He is, as it were, morning by morning inspecting our stores, that accordingly He may send help. Greater and more manifest nearness of the Lord's presence I have never had, than when after breakfast there were no means for dinner, and then the Lord provided the dinner for more than one hundred persons; or when, after dinner, there were no means for tea, and yet the Lord provided the tea; and all this without one single human being having been informed about our need.

This moreover I add: that although we, who have been eye-witnesses of these gracious interpositions of our Father, have not been so benefited by them as we might and ought to have been, yet we have in some measure derived blessings from them. One thing is certain, that we are not tired of doing the Lord's work in this way.

When the south wind blew

Müller was a good story-teller. In the fifth part of his *Narratives*, published in 1874, he vividly described a remarkable incident which also illustrates how he combined faith with resourcefulness and common sense. At a time of crisis, he says, doing nothing would be the 'counterfeit of faith'.

It was towards the end of November of 1857 when I was most unexpectedly informed that the boiler of our heating apparatus at number one [children's home on Ashley Down] leaked very considerably, so that it was impossible to go through the winter with such a leak.

Our heating apparatus consists of a large cylinder boiler, inside of which the fire is kept, and with which boiler the water pipes that warm the rooms are connected. Hot air is also connected to this apparatus.

The boiler had been considered suited for the work of the winter. To suspect that it was worn out, and not to do anything towards replacing it by a new one, and to have said, I will trust in God regarding it, would be careless presumption, but not faith in God. It would be the counterfeit of faith.

The boiler is entirely surrounded by brickwork; its state therefore could not be known without taking down the brickwork; this, if needless, would be rather injurious to the boiler than otherwise; and as for eight winters we had had no difficulty in this way, we had not anticipated it now. But suddenly, and most unexpectedly, at the commencement of the winter, this difficulty occurred.

What then was to be done? For the children, especially the younger infants, I felt deeply concerned that they might not suffer through want of warmth. But how were we to obtain warmth?

The introduction of a *new* boiler would in all probability

take many weeks. The *repairing* of the boiler was a questionable matter, on account of the greatness of the leak; but, if not, nothing could be said of it, till the brick-chamber in which it is enclosed was, at least in part, removed; but that would, at least as far as we could judge, take days; and what was to be done in the meantime to find warm rooms for three hundred children?

It naturally occurred to me to introduce temporary gas-stoves; but on further weighing the matter, it was found that we should be unable to heat our very large rooms with gas, except we had many stoves, which we could not introduce, as we had not a sufficient quantity of gas to spare from our lighting apparatus. Moreover, from each of these stoves we needed a small chimney to carry off the impure air. This mode of heating therefore, though applicable to a hall, a staircase, or a shop, would not suit our purpose.

I also thought of the temporary introduction of Arnott's stoves; but they would have been unsuitable, requiring long chimneys (as they would have been of a temporary kind) to go out of the windows. On this account, the uncertainty of their answering in our case, and the disfigurement of the rooms, led me to give up this plan also.

But what was to be done? Gladly would I have paid a hundred pounds if thereby the difficulty could have been overcome, and the children not be exposed to suffer for many days from being in cold rooms.

At last I determined on falling entirely into the hands of God, Who is very merciful and of tender compassion, and I decided on having the brick-chamber opened to see the extent of the damage, and whether the boiler might be repaired so as to carry us through the winter.

The day was fixed when the workmen were to come, and all the necessary arrangements were made. The fire of course had to be let out while the repairs were going on. But now see. After the day was fixed for the repairs, a bleak north wind set in. It began to blow either on Thursday or Friday before the Wednesday afternoon when the fire was to be let out. Now came the first really cold weather which we had in the beginning of that winter, during the first days of December. What was to be done? The repairs could not be put off.

I now asked the Lord for two things: that He would be

pleased to change the north wind into a south wind, and that he would give the workmen 'a mind to work'; for I remembered how much Nehemiah accomplished in fifty-two days, whilst building the walls of Jerusalem, because 'the people had a mind to work'.

Well, the memorable day came. The evening before, the bleak north wind blew still; but, on the Wednesday, the south wind blew; exactly as I had prayed. The weather was so mild that no fire was needed. The brickwork is removed, the leak is found out very soon, the boiler makers begin to repair in good earnest.

About half past eight in the evening, when I was going home, I was informed at the lodge that the acting principal of the firm, whence the boiler makers came, had arrived to see how the work was going on, and whether he could in any way speed the matter.

I went immediately therefore into the cellar to see him with the men, to seek to expedite the business. In speaking to the principal of this, he said in their hearing, 'The men will work late this evening, and come very early again tomorrow.'

'We would rather, Sir,' said the leader, 'work all night.'

Then remembered I the second part of my prayer, that God would give the men 'a mind to work'.

Thus it was: by the morning the repair was accomplished, the leak was stopped, though with great difficulty, and within about thirty hours the brick-work was up again and the fire in the boiler; and all the time the south wind blew so mildly, that there was not the least need of a fire.

Here, then, is one of our difficulties which was overcome by prayer and faith.

3

In touch with God

A look at Müller's prayer life

Knowing the heart of God

'True prayer,' wrote Bishop Westcott, a contemporary of Müller's, '– the prayer that must be answered – is the personal recognition and acceptance of the divine will.' Müller agreed. The heading of this section is taken from a passage in the third part of his *Narratives*, published in 1845, towards the end of the period when he experienced his greatest trials of faith.

From the beginning when God put this service into my heart I had anticipated trials and straits; but knowing, as I did, the heart of God, through the experience of several years previously, I also knew that He would listen to the prayers of His child who trusts in Him, and that He would not leave him in the hour of need, but listen to his prayers and deliver him out of the difficulty.

Commenting on a succession of answers to prayer recorded in his journal for the 1830s, and later reproduced in his *Narratives*, Müller wrote (in 1837):

In reading about all these answers to prayer, the believing reader may be led to think that I am spiritually minded above most of the children of God, and that therefore the Lord favours us thus. The true reason is this. Just in as many points as we are acting according to the mind of God, in so many are we blessed and made a blessing.

Our manner of living is according to the mind of the Lord, for He delights in seeing His children thus come to Him (Matt. 6); and therefore though I am weak and erring in many points, yet He blesses me in this particular, and, I doubt not, will bless me as long as He shall enable me to act according to His will in this matter.

In a little tract entitled 'How to ascertain the will of God' Müller wrote:

I seek at the beginning to get my heart in such a state that it has no will of its own in regard to a given matter. Nine tenths of the trouble with people generally is just here. Nine tenths of the difficulties are overcome when our hearts are ready to do the Lord's will, whatever it may be. When one is truly in this state, it is usually but a little way to the knowledge of what His will is.

Having done this, I do not leave the result to feeling or simple impression. If so, I make myself liable to great delusions.

I seek the will of the Spirit of God through, or in connection with, the Word of God. The Spirit and the Word must be combined. If I look to the Spirit alone without the Word, I lay myself open to great delusions also. If the Holy Spirit guides us at all, He will do it according to the Scriptures and never contrary to them.

Next I take into account providential circumstances. These often plainly indicate God's will in connection with His Word and Spirit.

I ask God in prayer to reveal His will to me aright.

Thus through prayer to God, the study of the Word, and reflection, I come to a deliberate judgment according to the best of my ability and knowledge; and if my mind is thus at peace, and continues so after two or three more petitions, I proceed accordingly. In trivial matters, and in transactions involving most important issues, I have found this method always effective.

This process took time. In 1833, before he had embarked on his children's work, Müller seriously considered going as a missionary to Baghdad. He did not go, but these extracts from his journal are typical of the way in which Müller got to know the mind and heart of God.

January 5. I considered with brother Craik [his co-pastor at Bethesda chapel] about going to Baghdad. We see nothing clearly. If the Lord will have me go, here I am.

January 7. I spent again some time in prayer, respecting our going to Baghdad, and examined more fully into it.

January 8. I had from half past five till eight this morning to myself in prayer and reading the Word. I prayed then, and repeatedly besides this day, respecting our going to Baghdad. I wrote also a letter to some believers at Barnstaple to ask their prayers concerning this matter. I do not see more clearly than I did before.

January 9. I again asked the Lord concerning Baghdad, but see nothing clearly respecting it. I told the Lord I should stay at my post unless He Himself should most evidently take me away, and I did not feel afterwards my remaining here to be against His will.

January 14. I feel more and more satisfied that it is not of the Lord that I should go to Baghdad.

January 19. For some days past I have been reading brother Groves' journal of his residence at Baghdad, both for the sake of information respecting his position there, and also, if it please the Lord, that He may use this as a means to show me clearly whether I should go or stay. Blessed be His name that I have no desire of my own in this matter!

In the early days of his work, Müller cared for his children in rented homes in Wilson Street, Bristol. Then, in 1849, he opened a large purpose-built home for three hundred children at a beautiful site on Ashley Down on the outskirts of the town. By the end of 1850, he was already considering building again on an adjoining site and more than doubling the size of his work. Such an expansion would cost thousands of pounds. On 15 December, 1850, he wrote in his journal:

The especial burden of my prayer is that God would be pleased to teach me His will. My mind has also been especially pondering how I could know His will satisfactorily concerning this particular. Sure I am that I shall be taught. I therefore desire patiently to wait for the Lord's time, when He shall be pleased to shine on my path concerning this point.

On 26 December he recorded:

Every day since the 5 December I have continued to pray about this matter, and that with a goodly measure of earnestness by the help of God. There has passed scarcely an hour during these days, in which, whilst awake, this matter has not been more or less before me. But all without even a shadow of excitement. I converse with no one about it. Hitherto have I not even done so with my dear wife. From this I refrain still, and deal with God alone about the matter, in order that no outward influence, and no outward excitement may keep me from attaining unto a clear discovery of His will. I have the fullest and most peaceful assurance, that He will clearly show me His will.

This evening I have had again an especial solemn reason for prayer, to seek to know the will of God. But whilst I continue to entreat and beseech the Lord that He would not allow me to be deluded in this business, I may say I have scarcely any doubt remaining in my mind as to what will be the issue, even that I should go forward in this matter. As this, however, is one of the most momentous steps that I have ever taken, I judge that I cannot go about this matter with too much caution, prayerfulness, and deliberation. I am in no hurry about it. I could wait for years, by God's grace, were this His will, before even taking one single step towards this thing, or even speaking to anyone about it; and, on the other hand, I would set to work tomorrow, were the Lord to bid me to do so. This calmness of mind, this having no will of my own in the matter, this only wishing to please my Heavenly Father in it, this only seeking His and not my honour in it; this state of heart, I say, is the fullest assurance to me that my heart is not under a fleshly excitement, and that, if helped thus to go on, I shall know the will of God to the full.

But, while I write thus, I cannot but add, at the same time, that I do crave the honour and the glorious privilege to be more and more used by the Lord. I have served Satan much in my younger years, and desire now with all my might to serve God during the remaining days of my earthly pilgrimage. I am forty-five years and three months old. Every day decreases the number of days that I have to stay on earth. I therefore desire with all my might to work. There are vast multitudes of orphans to be provided for. About five years ago, a brother in the Lord told me he had seen in an official report that there were at that time six thousand young orphans in the prisons of England. My heart longs to be instrumental in preventing such young orphans from having to go to prison.

And before he opened his third children's home, in 1862, Müller prayed about this expansion *every day* for more than eleven years.

God at work

Müller would not have agreed that the phrase 'knowing the heart of God' was a sufficient definition of prayer. There was more to it than that: the process was two-way, and God intervened to work in the hearts of His people. In 1861, Müller wrote:

I ask God to influence the hearts of those who know of the work through the reports or otherwise to help me with their means; and He does so.

More specifically he recorded that:

Every Wednesday evening I meet with my helpers for united prayer; and day by day I have stated seasons when I seek to bring the work with all its great variety of spiritual and temporal necessities before the Lord in prayer having perhaps each day fifty or more matters to bring before Him, and thus I obtain the blessing.

Making needs known only to God

We have said that Müller never appealed for funds, or asked individuals to help him. Sceptics sometimes said to him:

'There is no difference between your way of proceeding, on the one hand, and going from individual to individual asking them for means on the other; for the writing of reports [which Müller did, see page 77] is just the same thing.'

His reply was:

There is a great difference. Suppose that we are in need. Suppose that our poverty lasts for some weeks or even some months together. Is there not in that case a difference between asking the Lord only from day to day, without speaking to any human being not connected directly with the work, about our poverty on the one hand; and writing letters or making personal application to benevolent individuals for assistance on the other hand?

Truly there is a great difference between these two modes. I do not mean to say that it would be acting against the precepts of the Lord to seek for help in His work by personal and individual application to *believers* (though it would be in direct opposition to His will to apply to *unbelievers*: 2 Cor. 6:14–18); but *I* act in the way in which I do for the benefit of the Church at large, cheerfully bearing the trials, and sometimes the deep trials, connected with the life of faith (which however brings along with it also its precious joys), if by any means a part at least of my fellow believers might be led to see the reality of dealing with God only, and that there is such a thing as the child of God having power with God by prayer and faith.

That the Lord should use for so glorious a service one so vile, so unfaithful, so altogether unworthy of the least notice as I am, I can only ascribe to the riches of His condescending grace in which He takes up the most unlikely instruments that the honour may be manifestly His.

I add only one word more: should Satan seek to whisper into your ears: Perhaps the matter is made known after all when there is a need, I reply: Whom did I ask for anything these many years since the work has been going on? To whom did I make known our wants, except to those who are closely connected with the work?

So, far from wishing to make known our need, for the purpose of influencing benevolent persons to contribute to the necessities of the institution under my care, I have even refused to let our circumstances be known, after having been asked about them, when on simply saying that we were in need, I might have had considerable sums. In such cases I refused in order that the hand of God only might be manifest; for that, and not the money, nor even the ability of continuing to carry on the work, is my especial aim. And such self-possession has the Lord given me, that at the times of the deepest poverty (whilst there was nothing at all in hand, and whilst we had even from meal to meal to wait upon the Lord for the necessities of more than 100 persons), when a donation of five pounds or ten pounds or more has been given to me, the donors could not have read in my countenance whether we had much or nothing at all in hand.

An amusing exchange of letters well illustrates Müller's determination to make his needs known only to God. In a letter dated 17 March, 1840, the writer – who had several times previously sent donations to Müller – asked him:

Have you any present need for the institution under your care? I know you do not *ask*, except indeed of Him whose work you are doing; but to *answer when asked* seems another thing, and a right thing. I have a reason for desiring to know the present state of your means towards the objects you are labouring to serve: viz. should you not have need, other departments of the Lord's work or other people of the Lord may have need. Kindly then inform me, and to what amount, i.e. what amount you at this present time need, or can profitably lay out.

Müller certainly was in need when the letter arrived. He was on the point of establishing an infant school; he needed Bibles to continue his literature distribution; and his orphan-fund amounted to a grand total of just over two shillings. His reply however was as follows:

Whilst I thank you for your love, and whilst I agree with you that, in general, there is a difference between *asking for money*, and *answering when asked*, nevertheless in our case I feel not at liberty to speak about the state of our funds, as the primary object of the work in my hands is to lead those who are weak in faith to see that there is *reality* in dealing with God *alone*.

But having despatched the letter, Müller had no hesitation in praying:

'Lord, You know that for Your sake I did not tell this brother

about our need. Now, Lord, show afresh that there is reality
in speaking to You only about our need, and speak therefore
to this brother so that he may help us.'

The prayer was answered. Müller received a hundred pounds
from the writer of the letter who was apparently not offended
by the reply he had received. The infant school was
established, the extra Bibles ordered, and the children
supplied for another week.

'The hearts of all men at His disposal'

So while Müller never appealed for money, he had no
scruples whatsoever about asking God to influence individuals to give to his work. It sometimes happened that such
people were actually conscious of God working in their
hearts. One example of this is recorded in Müller's journal for
1865.

July 25. From the neighbourhood of London a hundred
pounds, with the following letter:
   'My dear Sir, I believe that it is through the Lord's acting
upon me, that I enclose you a cheque on the Bank of England,
Western Branch, for a hundred pounds. I hope that your
affairs are going on well.'
   This Christian gentleman, whom I have never seen, and
who is engaged in a very large business in London, had sent
me several times before a similar sum. A day or two before I
received this last kind donation, I had asked the Lord that He
would be pleased to influence the heart of this donor to help
me again, which I had never done before regarding him; and
thus I had the double answer to prayer, in that not only
money came in, but money from *him*.

In his *Narratives*, Müller commented:

Perhaps the reader may think that, in acknowledging the
receipt of this donation, I wrote to the donor what I have

stated in my journal. I did not. My reason for not doing so was lest he should have thought I was in especial need, and might have been thus influenced to send more. In truly knowing the Lord, in really relying upon Him and upon Him alone, there is no need of giving hints directly or indirectly whereby individuals may be induced further to help. I might have written to the donor (as was indeed the case): I need a considerable sum day by day for the current expenses of the various objects of the institution, and also might have with truth told him at that time that I yet needed about twenty thousand pounds to meet all the expenses connected with the contemplated enlargement of the orphan work. But my practice is never to allude to any of these things in my correspondence with donors. When the report is published everyone can see, who has a desire to see, how matters stand; and thus I leave things in the hands of God to speak for us to the hearts of His stewards. And this He does. Verily we do not wait upon God in vain!

Müller wrote in 1875:

Our Heavenly Father has the hearts of all men at His disposal, and we give ourselves to prayer to Him, and He, in answer to our prayers, lays the necessities of this work on the hearts of His stewards; and thus it has come to pass that we have now received from Him, in answer to prayer, more than seven hundred thousand pounds

Should anyone question this statement, we reply, Whom did we ask for anything? Let the individuals come forward to prove that it is otherwise. Nothing could be easier than to unmask me as a deceiver, an imposter, or a hypocrite. But if this cannot be done, as it cannot, then will not the reader see how much power there is in believing prayer, and how much may be obtained through the exercise of faith? Though the real power of prayer is by certain individuals denied, yet the orphan houses on Ashley Down, erected at a cost of about one hundred and fifteen thousand pounds, without anyone being asked for anything, but God only, plainly shows that even in the latter part of the nineteenth century much may be obtained from our Heavenly Father simply through prayer and faith.

The test of patience

Later in his life, Müller looked back on the period from 1838 to 1846 as the time when he had experienced his greatest trials of faith in his children's work. They were not years of continuous difficulty: rather there tended to be a pattern of a few months of trial followed by some months of comparative plenty. During the whole period Müller insisted that the children knew nothing of the trial. In the midst of one of the darkest periods, he recorded, 'These dear little ones know nothing about it, because their tables are as well supplied as when there was eight hundred pounds in the bank, and they have lack of nothing.'

The periods of trial were so in the sense that there was no excess of funds: God supplied the need by the day, even by the hour. Enough was sent, but no more than enough. These years appear to have been a test of Müller's obedience: a time when his character was moulded and prepared for his life's work. In the opinion of the present director of the Müller Homes, the years were 'designed by the Lord to deepen Mr Müller's faith and to show him that prayer is no vain thing. Many years afterwards he faced his financial trials with scarcely a tremor. He had learned so much and really knew his God.'

During this period, Müller made two short visits to Germany to work in a small Baptist church. During his second visit, a lesser man might have been tempted to break the rule about never revealing the state of the funds. For, as he recorded in his journal, there were those who said:

'We are quite sure there must be much money in hand for the orphans, else Mr Müller would not have gone to Germany.'

This was by no means the case, and Müller observed later that:

Often have I had similar things said to me, or about the work, when we have been in the deepest poverty, simply because in faith a certain step had been taken, or a certain thing had been done, which was connected with great expense. At such times, of course, my fellow-labourers and I have had to be silent. For we could not say it was not so, else it would be exposing our poverty, and would look like asking for help. Therefore we have had to be content with something like this:

'Lord, it is said that there is much money in hand, whereby some who would otherwise help us, it may be, are kept from doing so; now, Lord, do Thou nevertheless, as the work is Thine, lay our need, the real state of things, on the hearts of Thy children that they may help us.'

Thus it was during my service in Germany in the summer of 1845 also. My fellow-labourers in Bristol and my dear wife and I in Stuttgart poured out our hearts before the Lord, seeking His help upon the work, and asking Him also for means, and He did not despise our cries. There came in, during the twelve weeks that I was away, for the orphans alone, two hundred pounds, five shillings and fivepence ha'penny. This, together with what was in hand when I left, and with some money that at the end of my stay in Germany I could order to be drawn out of my bankers' hands in Bristol, richly supplied all the need during my absence. But the labourers were repeatedly in straits, and several times the last money was gone; but the Lord refreshed their hearts by seasonable help.

An even greater test of Müller's faith occurred in 1851 when he was planning to build his second children's home on Ashley Down.

October 2. Evening. Nothing has come in today for the building fund, and very little during the last ten days. I have had just now again a long season for prayer respecting this object. Through the support which I receive from the Lord, I am not cast down, though only so little as yet has come in. The work is His, and not mine; therefore I am able quietly to leave it in His hands. Were I to look at what has come in hitherto, much though it is in one sense, it would take, after this rate, about ten years before I should have the sum needed; but this does not cast me down; for when the Lord's time is come I expect larger sums.

Further, there are peculiar natural obstacles in the way to my receiving donations for this object; for it has now been several months reported that I have already thirty thousand pounds in hand for the building fund, though this day it is actually only one thousand one hundred and thirty-nine pounds, nineteen shillings and twopence ha'penny. Again and again this has been told me, and therefore were I to look at things naturally I should have much reason to be cast down, as the spread of such reports is calculated humanly speaking to keep persons from contributing towards this object. Another class of persons, true Christians, and liberal persons too, may be thinking that the sum required is so large that it is not likely I shall obtain it, and that therefore their contributing towards this object would be useless.

But none of these things discourages me. God knows that I have not thirty thousand pounds in hand. God can influence the minds of His dear children towards this intended orphan-house, whatever their thoughts may have been hitherto on the subject.

I therefore seek to 'let patience have her perfect work', and go on in prayer, being fully assured that the Lord will not suffer me to be confounded. I am day by day looking out for help, yea, for large sums; and I know I shall have them after the Lord has exercised my faith and patience. Lord wilt Thou mercifully continue to give unto Thy servant faith and patience!

Doing things God's way

We have seen that Müller thought that to do nothing at a time of crisis was the 'counterfeit of faith'. But at the same time he was always careful to avoid the temptation to work out his own solutions to problems which he had brought to God in prayer. During a difficult time in 1838 he recorded in his journal:

September 8. Saturday evening. I am still in the hour of probation. It has not pleased my gracious Lord to send me help as yet. The evening before last I heard brother Craik preach on Genesis 12 about Abraham's faith. He showed how all went on well as long as Abraham acted in faith, and walked according to the will of God; and how all failed when he distrusted God.

I felt it particularly important in my own case that I may not go any by-ways, or ways of my own, for deliverance. I have about two hundred and twenty pounds in the bank, which, for other purposes in the Lord's work, has been entrusted to me by a brother and a sister. I might take of this money, and say but to the sister, and write but to the brother, that I have taken, in these my straits, twenty pounds, fifty pounds or a hundred pounds for the orphans, and they would be quite satisfied (for both of them have liberally given for the orphans, and the brother has more than once told me only to let him know when I wanted money); but this would be a deliverance of my own, not God's deliverance. Besides, it would be no small barrier to the exercise of faith in the next hour of trial.

Arguing with God

At the beginning of the period of eight years trial (page 50) Müller recorded:

I have been pleading with God eleven arguments why He should be graciously pleased to send help ... The arguments which I plead with God are:

That I set about the work for the glory of God, i.e. that there might be a visible proof, by God supplying, in answer to prayer only, the necessities of the orphans, that He is the living God, and most willing, even in our day, to answer prayer; and that therefore He would be pleased to send supplies.

That God is the 'Father of the fatherless', and that He therefore, as their Father, would be pleased to provide. Psalm 68:5.

That I have received the children in the name of Jesus, and that therefore He, in these children, has been received, and is fed, and is clothed; and that therefore He would be pleased to consider this. Mark 9: 36–37.

That the faith of many of the children of God has been

strengthened by this work hitherto, and that, if God were to withhold the means for the future, those who are weak in faith would be staggered; whilst by a continuance of means their faith might still further be strengthened.

That many enemies would laugh were the Lord to withhold supplies, and say, 'Did we not foretell that this enthusiasm would come to nothing?'

That many of the children of God who are uninstructed, or in a carnal state, would feel themselves *justified* to continue their alliance with the world in the work of God, and to go on as heretofore, in their unscriptural proceedings respecting similar institutions, so far as obtaining means is concerned, if He were not to help me.

That the Lord would remember that I am His child, and that He would graciously pity me, and remember that *I* cannot provide for these children, and that therefore He would not allow this burden to lie upon me long without sending help.

That He would remember likewise my fellow-labourers in the work, who trust in Him, but who would be tried were He to withhold supplies.

That He would remember that I should have to dismiss the children from under our scriptural instruction to their former companions.

That He would show that those were mistaken who said that, *at the first*, supplies might be expected while the thing was new, but not afterwards.

That I should not know, were He to withhold means, what construction I should put on all the many remarkable answers to prayer which He had given me heretofore in connexion with this work, and which most fully have shown to me that it is of God.

In some small measure I now understand, experimentally, the meaning of that word, 'how long', which so frequently occurs in the prayers of the Psalms. But even now, by the grace of God, my eyes are up unto Him only, and I believe that He will send help.

God's answers

God did send help of course, as the extracts from Müller's journal in this section show. As a guide to the value of money, remember that through most of the nineteenth century a farm labourer earned about ten shillings (fifty pence) a week. In the 1830s and 40s, Müller could look after one hundred children for two or three pounds a day.

February 13, 1839. This afternoon I paid out the last money which we had in hand, and giving it to brother T said, We have now again to look to the Lord for further supplies. This evening five pounds was given to me, which had come in under the following circumstances. A gentleman and lady visited the orphan-houses, and met at the boys' orphan-house two ladies who were likewise visiting. One of the ladies said to the matron of the boys' orphan-house: 'Of course, you cannot carry on these institutions without a good stock of funds.'

The gentleman, turning to the matron, said: 'Have you a good stock?'

She replied: 'Our funds are deposited in a bank which cannot break.'

Tears came into the eyes of the inquiring lady. The gentleman, on leaving, gave to the master of the boys five pounds, which came in *when I had not a penny in hand*.

July 15, 1839. Monday. Today two pounds, seven shillings and threepence was needed for the orphans, but we had nothing. How to obtain the means for a dinner, and for what else was needed, I knew not. My heart was perfectly at peace, and unusually sure of help, though I knew not in the least whence it was to come.

Before brother T came, I received a letter from India, written in May, with an order for fifty pounds for the orphans. I had said last Saturday to brother T that it would be desirable to have fifty pounds, as the salaries of all my fellow-labourers are due, the treacle casks empty, all the provision stores exhausted, several articles of clothing needed, and worsted for the boys to go on with their knitting. Now the Lord has sent exactly fifty pounds. Moreover this money comes very seasonably, as in three days I shall have to leave

Bristol for some days, and can now go comfortably, as it regards leaving means behind.

November 11, 1839. Monday morning. Yesterday, when there was not a penny in hand, there was given to me, with Ecclesiastes 9:10, ten shillings. This morning came in one pound, ten shillings. Soon afterwards a note was sent to me from the orphan-houses, to say that the need of today would be three pounds. Just while I was reading the note I received another, including a sovereign, which a sister from Devonshire had given to one of the brethren for the orphans. Thus I had just the three pounds which was needed. A few minutes after came in one shilling more.

December 2, 1839. Since the last money has been given out for housekeeping, only one pound, twelve shillings has come in; but as one pound, ten shillings of this had been given for the rents, I had only two shillings in hand, when brother B, the master of the boys' orphan-house, came this morning and told me that the need of today would be at least two pounds. I gave him the two shillings which I had, and proposed that we should pray together for more means. While we were in prayer, a brother called. After prayer brother B left me, and the brother who had come gave me five pounds. As soon as he had left, I went joyfully with the money to the orphan-houses, to prevent the bakers being sent away. This evening I received still further two pounds. Thus the Lord has richly supplied our need for today and tomorrow.

Commenting on the way God answered his prayers in these years, Müller said:

Particularly notice that the help never comes too late. We may be poor, yea, very poor; yet the help comes at the right time. We may have to wait upon the Lord, yea, even a long time; but at last He helps. It may seem as if the Lord had forgotten us by leaving us very poor, and very poor, and that week after week; but at last He helps abundantly, and shows that only for the trial of our faith, both for our own benefit and the benefit of those who might hear of His dealings with us, has He allowed us to call so long upon Him.

In later years, Müller received larger gifts.

January 4, 1853. I received today the promise that, as the joint donation of several Christians, there should be paid to me a donation of eight thousand and one hundred pounds for the work of the Lord in my hands. Of this sum I propose to take six thousand pounds for the building fund, six hundred pounds for the current expenses of the orphans, and fifteen hundred pounds for the current objects of the Scriptural Knowledge Institution.

It is impossible to describe the spiritual refreshment which my heart received through this donation. Day by day, for nineteen months, I had been looking out for more abundant help than I had had. I was fully assured that God would help me with larger sums; yet the delay was long. See how precious it is to wait upon God! See how those who do so are not confounded! Their faith and patience may long and sharply be tried; but in the end it will most assuredly be seen that those who honour God, He will honour, and will not suffer them to be put to shame. The largeness of the donation, whilst it exceedingly refreshed my spirit, did not in the least surprise me; for I expect great things from God.

In 1856, Müller made an important statement with which we may conclude our look at his prayer life.

Never since the orphan work has been in existence have I asked one single human being for any help for this work; and yet, unasked for, simply in answer to prayer, from so many parts of the world the donations have come in, and that very frequently at a time of the greatest need. Were I to state what is not true, persons could easily convict me; to say nothing of the fact that God, whose name I have continually connected with this work, would disown me as an awful deceiver, and bring this work to nought; but if these things are true, as indeed they are, will not my readers recognise the minute particular providence of God, and the readiness of His heart to listen to the supplications of those who come to Him with their requests in the name of the Lord Jesus? I do not seek a name for myself in connexion with this work; I do not wish to draw attention to myself, and am indeed sorry when persons have had their attention directed only to me; but I do seek honour for my Heavenly Father, and I do desire that His hand may be owned in this work.

4

Listening to God

Müller and the Bible

God speaking to us

In a letter he wrote to the British and Foreign Bible Society towards the end of his life, Müller said that he had read the whole Bible through 'considerably more than one hundred times ... with prayer and meditation'.

Speaking about the importance of Bible reading to his own congregation at Bethesda Chapel in Bristol in May, 1871, he said:

I judge that though prayer is of the utmost moment, yet still this is as deeply, or more deeply important than prayer itself: for when we pray to God, we speak to God; but when we read the Scriptures God speaks to us, and this is what we so much need.

A transforming discovery

In the spring of 1841, Müller spent seven weeks with his family at Nailsworth in the Cotswold Hills. He busied himself while preparing the second part of his *Narratives* for publication, in preaching and pastoral work. It was during this time, that he made a discovery about his daily quiet time with God which transformed his spiritual life. He described his new insight like this:

I saw more clearly than ever that the first great and primary business to which I ought to attend every day was *to have my soul happy in the Lord*. The first thing to be concerned about was not how much I might serve the Lord, or how I might glorify the Lord; but how I might get my soul into a happy state, and how my inner man might be nourished. For I might seek to set the truth before the unconverted, I might seek to benefit believers, I might seek to relieve the distressed, I might in other ways seek to behave myself as it becomes a child of God in this world; and yet, not being happy in the Lord, and not being nourished and strengthened in my inner man day by day, all this might not be attended to in a right spirit.

Before this time my practice had been, at least for ten years previously, as an habitual thing, to give myself to prayer after having dressed myself in the morning. *Now*, I saw that the most important thing I had to do was to give myself to the reading of the Word of God, and to meditation on it, that thus my heart might be comforted, encouraged, warned, reproved, instructed; and that thus, by means of the Word of God, whilst meditating on it, my heart might be brought into experimental communion with the Lord.

I began therefore to meditate on the New Testament from the beginning, early in the morning. The first thing I did, after having asked in a few words the Lord's blessing upon His precious Word, was to begin to meditate on the Word of God, searching as it were into every verse to get blessing out of it; not for the sake of the public ministry of the Word, not for the sake of preaching on what I had meditated upon, but for the sake of obtaining food for my own soul.

The result I have found to be almost invariably this, that after a very few minutes my soul has been led to confession, or to thanksgiving, or to intercession, or to supplication; so that, though I did not, as it were, give myself to prayer, but to meditation, yet it turned almost immediately more or less into prayer. When thus I have been for a while making confession or intercession or supplication, or have given thanks, I go on to the next words or verse, turning all, as I go on, into prayer for myself or others, as the Word may lead to it, but still continually keeping before me that food for my own soul is the object of my meditation. The result of this is that there is always a good deal of confession, thanksgiving, supplication, or intercession mingled with my meditation, and that my inner man almost invariably is even sensibly nourished and strengthened, and that by breakfast time, with rare exceptions, I am in a peaceful if not happy state of heart.

Thus also the Lord is pleased to communicate unto me that which, either very soon after or at a later time, I have found to become food for other believers, though it was not for the sake of the public ministry of the Word that I gave myself to meditation, but for the profit of my own inner man.

With this mode I have likewise combined being out in the open air for an hour, an hour and a half, or two hours, before breakfast, walking about in the fields, and in the summer sitting for a little on the stiles, if I find it too much to walk all the time. I find it very beneficial to my health to walk thus for meditation before breakfast, and am now so in the habit of using the time for that purpose, that when I get into the open air I generally take out a New Testament of good-sized type, which I carry with me for that purpose, besides my Bible; and I find that I can profitably spend my time in the open air, which formerly was not the case for want of habit. I used to consider the time spent in walking a loss, but now I find it very profitable, not only to my body but also to my soul. The walking out before breakfast is, of course, not necessarily connected with this matter, and everyone has to judge according to his strength and other circumstances.

The difference, then, between my former practice and my present one is this: formerly, when I rose, I began to pray as soon as possible, and generally spent all my time till breakfast in prayer, or almost all the time. At all events I almost invariably began with prayer, except when I felt my soul to be more than usually barren, in which case I read the Word of God for food, or for refreshment, or for a revival and renewal of my inner man, before I gave myself to prayer. But what was the result? I often spent a quarter of an hour, or half an hour, or even an hour on my knees before being conscious to myself of having derived comfort, encouragement, humbling of soul, etc.; and often, after having suffered much from wandering of mind for the first ten minutes, or quarter of an hour, or even half an hour, I only then really began to pray.

I scarcely ever suffer now in this way. For my heart being nourished by the truth, being brought into *experimental* fellowship with God, I speak to my Father and to my Friend (vile though I am, and unworthy of it) about the things that He has brought before me in His precious Word. It often now astonishes me that I did not sooner see this point. In no book did I ever read about it. No public ministry ever brought the matter before me. No private conversation with a brother stirred me up to this matter. And yet now, since God has taught me this point, it is as plain to me as anything that the first thing the child of God has to do morning by morning is to *obtain food for his inner man*. As the outward man is not fit for work for any length of time except we take food, and as this is one of the first things we do in the morning, so it should be with the inner man. We should take food for that, as everyone must allow.

Now what is the food for the inner man? Not prayer, but the Word of God; and here again, not the simple reading of the Word of God, so that it only passes through our minds, just as water passes through a pipe, but considering what we read, pondering over it and applying it to our hearts.

When we pray we speak to God. Now prayer, in order to be continued for any length of time in any other than a formal manner, requires, generally speaking, a measure of strength or godly desire, and the season therefore when this exercise of the soul can be most effectually performed is after the inner man has been nourished by meditation on the Word of God, where we find our Father speaking to us, to encourage us, to comfort us, to instruct us, to humble us, to reprove us. We may therefore profitably meditate with God's blessing though we are ever so weak spiritually; nay, the weaker we are, the more we need meditation for the strengthening of our inner man. Thus there is far less to be feared from wandering of mind than if we give ourselves to prayer without having had time previously for meditation.

I dwell so particularly on this point because of the immense spiritual profit and refreshment I am conscious of having derived from it myself, and I affectionately and solemnly beseech all my fellow believers to ponder this matter. By the blessing of God, I ascribe to this mode the help and strength which I have had from God to pass in peace through deeper trials, in various ways, than I have ever had before; and having now above fourteen years tried this way, I can most fully, in the fear of God, commend it.

How to read the Bible

Over thirty years later, in 1875, Müller spoke to a large

gathering of young Christians at the Mildmay Conference in London. His theme was the Word of God.

As one who for fifty years has known the Lord, and has laboured in word and doctrine, I ought to be able, in some little measure, to lend a helping hand to these younger believers. And if God will only condescend to use the acknowledgment of my own failures to which I refer, and of my experience, as a help to others in walking on the road to Heaven, I trust that your coming here will not be in vain. This was the very purpose of my leaving home – that I might help these dear young brethren.

One of the most deeply important points is that of attending to the careful, prayerful reading of the Word of God, and meditation thereon. I would therefore ask your particular attention to one verse in the Epistle of Peter (1 Pet. 2:1-3), where we are especially exhorted by the Holy Spirit through the apostle, regarding this subject. For the sake of the connexion, let us read the first verse: 'Wherefore laying aside all malice, and all guile and hypocrisies, and envies, and all evil-speakings, as new-born babes, desire the sincere milk of the Word, that ye may grow thereby; if so be ye have tasted that the Lord is gracious.'

The particular point to which I refer is contained in the second verse, 'as new-born babes, desire the sincere milk of the Word'. As growth in the natural life is attained by proper food, so in the spiritual life, if we desire to grow, this growth is only to be attained through the instrumentality of the Word of God. It is not stated here, as some might be very willing to say, that, 'The reading of the Word may be of importance under some circumstances.' Nor is it stated that you may gain profit by reading the statement which is made here; it is of the Word, and of the Word alone, that the apostle speaks, and nothing else.

You may say that the reading of this tract or of that book often does you good. I do not question it. Nevertheless the instrumentality which God has been specially pleased to appoint and to use is that of *the Word itself*; and just in the measure in which the disciples of the Lord Jesus attend to this, they will be strong in the Lord; and in so far as it is neglected, so far will they be weak. There is such a thing as babes being neglected, and what is the consequence? They never become healthy men or women, because of that early neglect.

Perhaps – and it is one of the most hurtful forms of this neglect – they obtain improper food, and therefore do not attain the full vigour of maturity. So with regard to the divine life. It is a most deeply important point, that we obtain right spiritual food at the very beginning of that life. What is that food? It is the *'sincere milk of the Word'*; that is the proper nourishment for the strengthening of the new life. Listen, then, my dear brethren and sisters, to some advice with regard to the Word.

First of all, it is of the utmost moment that we read regularly through the Scripture. We ought not to turn over the Bible, and pick out chapters as we please here and there, but we should read it carefully and regularly through. I speak advisedly, as one who has known the blessedness of thus reading the Word for the last forty-six years, because for the first four years of my Christian life I did not carefully read the Word of God. I used to read a tract, or an interesting book; but I knew nothing of the power of the Word. I read very little of it and the result was that, although a preacher then, yet I made very little progress in the divine life. And why? Just for this reason – I neglected the Word of God.

But it pleased God, through the instrumentality of a beloved Christian brother, to rouse in me an earnestness about the Word, and ever since then I have been a lover of it.

Let me then press upon you my first point, that of attending regularly to reading through the Scriptures. I do not suppose that you *all* need the exhortation. Many, I believe, have already done so; but I speak for the benefit of those who have not. To those I say, my dear friends, begin at once. Begin with the Old Testament, and when you have read a chapter or two, and are about to leave off, put a mark that you may know where you have left off. I speak in all simplicity for the benefit of those who may be young in the divine life. The next time you read, begin the New Testament, and again leave a mark where you leave off. And thus go on, always reading alternately the Old and New Testaments. Thus, by little and little, you will read through the whole Bible; and when you have finished, begin again at the beginning.

Why is this so deeply important? Simply that we may see *the connexion* between one book and another of the Bible, and between one chapter and another. If we do not read in this consecutive way, we lose a great part of what God has given to instruct us. Moreover, if we are children of God, we should be well acquainted with the whole revealed will of God – the whole of the Word. *'All Scripture is given by inspiration, and is profitable.'*

And much may be gained by thus carefully reading through the whole of the revealed will of God. Suppose a rich relative were to die, and leave us, perhaps, some land, or houses, or money, should we be content with reading only the clauses that affected us particularly? No, we would be careful to read the whole will right through. How much more then with regard to the revealed will of God ought we to be careful to read it through, and not merely one and another of the chapters or books.

And this careful reading of the Word of God has this advantage, that it keeps us from making *a system of doctrine of our own*, and from having our own particular favourite views, which is very pernicious. We often are apt to lay too much stress on certain views of the truth which affect us particularly. The will of the Lord is, that we should know *His whole revealed mind*. Again variety in the things of God is of great moment. And God has been pleased to give us this variety in the highest degree; and the child of God who follows out this plan will be able to take an interest in every part of the Word.

Suppose one says, 'Let us read in Leviticus.' Very well, my brother. Suppose another says, 'Let us read in the prophecy of Isaiah.' Very well, my brother. And another will say, 'Let us read in the Gospel according to Matthew.' Very well, my brother; I can enjoy them all; and whether it be in the Old Testament, or in the New Testament, whether in the Prophets, the Gospels, the Acts, or the Epistles, I should welcome it, and be delighted to welcome the reading and study of any part of the divine Word.

And this will be of particular advantage to us, in case we should become *labourers in Christ's vineyard*; because in expounding the Word, we shall be able to refer to every part of it. We shall equally enjoy the reading of the Word, whether of the Old or of the New Testament, and shall never get tired of it. I have, as I said before, known the blessedness of this plan for forty-six years, and though I am now nearly seventy years of age, and though I have been converted for nearly fifty years, I can say, by the grace of God, that I more than ever love the Word of God, and have greater delight than ever in reading it.

And though I have read the Word nearly a hundred times right through, I have never got tired of reading it, and this is more especially through reading it regularly, consecutively, day by day, and not merely reading a chapter here and there, as my own thoughts might have led me to do.

Again we should read the Scripture *prayerfully*, never supposing that we are clever enough or wise enough to understand God's Word by our own wisdom. In all our reading of the Scriptures let us seek carefully to have the help of the Holy Spirit; let us ask for Jesus' sake, that He will enlighten us. He is willing to do it.

The teaching of the Holy Spirit

Müller continued this sermon to his London audience of young people like this:

I will tell you how it fared with me at the very first; it may be for your encouragement. It was in the year 1829, when I was living in Hackney. My attention had been called to the teaching of the Spirit by a dear brother of experience. 'Well,' I said, 'I will try this plan; and will give myself, after prayer, to the careful reading of the Word of God, and to meditation, and I will see how much the Spirit is willing to teach me in this way.'

I went accordingly to my room, and locked my door, and putting the Bible on a chair, I went down on my knees at the chair. There I remained for several hours in prayer and meditation over the Word of God; and I can tell you that I learned more in those three hours which I spent in this way, than I had learned for many months previously. I thus obtained the teaching of the Divine Spirit, and I cannot tell you the blessedness which it was to my own soul. I was praying in the Spirit, and putting my trust in the power of the Spirit, as I had never done before.

You cannot therefore be surprised at my earnestness in pressing this upon you, when you have heard how precious to my heart it was, and how much it helped me.

But again, it is not enough to have prayerful reading only, but we must also *meditate* on the Word. As in the instance I have just referred to, kneeling before the chair I meditated on the Word. It was not simply reading it, not simply praying over it. It was all that, but, in addition it was *pondering over what I had read.* This is deeply important. If you merely read the Bible, and no more, it is just like water running in at one side and out at the other. *In order to be really benefited by it, we must meditate on it.* We cannot all of us, of course, spend many hours, or even one or two hours each day in this manner. Our business demands our attention. Yet however short the time you can afford, give it regularly to reading, prayer and meditation over the Word and you will find it will well repay you.

In connexion with this, we should always read and meditate over the Word of God with reference *to ourselves* and our own heart. This is deeply important, and I cannot press it too earnestly upon you. We are apt often to read the Word with reference to others. Parents read it in reference to their children, children for their parents; evangelists read it for their congregations, Sunday-school teachers for their classes. Oh! This is a poor way of reading the Word; if read in this way, it will not profit. I say it deliberately and advisedly, the sooner it is given up, the better for your own souls. Read the Word of God always with reference to your own heart, and when you have received the blessing in your own heart, you will be able to communicate it to others.

Whether you labour as evangelists, as pastors, or as visitors, superintendents of Sunday schools, or teachers, tract distributors, or in whatever other capacity you may seek to labour for the Lord, be careful to let the reading of the Word be with distinct reference to your own heart. Ask yourselves, how does this suit *me*, either for instruction, for correction, for exhortation, or for rebuke? How does this affect *me*? If you thus read, and get the blessing in your own soul, how soon will it flow out to others!

Another point. It is of the utmost moment in reading the Word of God, that the reading should be accompanied *with faith*. 'The Word preached did not profit them, not being mixed with faith in them that heard it.' As with the preaching, so with the reading it must be mixed with faith. Not simply reading it as you would read a story, which you may receive or not; not simply as a statement, which you may credit or not; or as an exhortation to which you may listen or not; but as the *revealed will of the Lord*: that is, receiving it *with faith*. Received thus, it will nourish us, and we shall reap benefit. Only in this way will it benefit us; and we shall gain from it health and strength in proportion as we receive it with real faith.

Lastly, if God does bless us in reading His Word, He expects that we should be *obedient* children, and that we should accept the Word as His will, and carry it into practice. If this be neglected, you will find that the reading of the Word, even if accompanied by prayer, meditation and faith, will do you little good. God does expect us to be obedient children, and will have us practise what He has taught us. The Lord Jesus Christ says: 'If you know these things, happy are ye *if ye do them*.' And in the measure in which we carry out what our Lord Jesus taught, so much in measure are we happy children. And in such measure only can we honestly look for help from our Father, even as we seek to carry out His will.

If there is one single point I would wish to have spread all over this country, and over the whole world, it is just this, that we should seek, beloved Christian friends, not to be hearers of the Word only, but 'doers of the Word'. I doubt not that many of you have sought to do this already, but I speak particularly to those younger brethren and sisters who have not yet learned the full force of this. Oh! Seek to attend earnestly to this, it is of vast importance. Satan will seek with much earnestness to put aside the Word of God; but let us seek to carry it out and to act upon it. The Word must be received as a legacy from God, which has been communicated to us by the Holy Spirit.

And remember that to the faithful reader of this blessed Word, it reveals all that we need to know about the Father, all that we need to know about the Lord Jesus Christ, and all about the power of the Spirit, all about the world that lieth in the wicked one, all about the road to Heaven, and the blessedness of the world to come. In this blessed book we have the whole gospel, and all rules necessary for our Christian life and warfare. Let us see then that we study it with our whole heart and with prayer, meditation, faith and obedience.

5

A Public Testimony

*Müller's view of himself
and his work*

All for God

Müller became a Christian at the age of twenty while a student at the University of Halle. In his *Narratives* he describes his life before his conversion as 'profligate and vicious' – there are vivid accounts of his heavy drinking (ten pints of beer in a single afternoon), theft, deception and a reference to 'gross immorality' shortly before his confirmation while a teenager. This style of life was interspersed by periods when he would try desperately hard to turn over a new leaf, and during these times he demonstrated his capacity for hard work by regularly rising at four and working through till ten at night. At Halle he studied theology under Friedrich Tholuck, left with a good degree, and later in life was able to speak and preach in seven languages. He also understood two or three oriental languages but did not claim to be master of them.

Four years after his conversion, during a stay in Devon in the summer of 1829 which brought him into contact with some of the founders of the Brethren movement, Müller experienced a change of outlook which he described as being 'like a second conversion'. In a letter written many years later, he referred to this time.

I became a believer in the Lord Jesus in the beginning of November, 1825 . . . For the first four years afterwards, it was for a good part in great weakness; but in July 1829 . . . it came with me to an entire and full surrender of heart. I gave myself fully to the Lord. Honour, pleasure, money, my physical powers, my mental powers, all was laid down at the feet of Jesus, and I became a great lover of the Word of God. I found my all in God.

Someone once asked him the secret of his service for God. He replied:

There was a day when I died, utterly died: died to George Müller, his opinions, preferences, tastes and will – died to the world, its approval or censure, died to the approval or blame even of my brethren and friends – and since then I have studied only to show myself approved unto God.

'Calm and calculating'

In 1851, Müller began to pray that God would give him the thirty-five thousand pounds which he estimated he would need to expand his work to care for one thousand children. Seven years later, he had received the required sum, and recorded in his *Narratives*:

Nearly seven years had I been, day by day, asking the Lord for the needed means to carry out the desire of my heart concerning the thousand orphans. Not a single day had elapsed since first I began to pray for means in which I had not been enabled, in the full assurance of faith that it would be granted, to bring my request before God, and generally I prayed more than once a day concerning this matter. When I began my request for means, viz. to entreat the Lord to give me thirty five thousand pounds, I knew well what difficulty there was in the way of my obtaining this sum, looking at it naturally. I am too calm, too calculating a person, too much in the habit of weighing all the difficulties of a case, to be carried away by excitement or imagination. I knew I had no ground *naturally* to expect this large sum.

His secret treasure

By the 1870s Müller's name had become a byword for faith in many countries. But while there were those who found him an inspiration, there were others who dismissed him as a fanatic. He was well aware of the criticisms which were levelled against him, and in 1874 he replied to them with some eloquence and wit.

We do not pretend to miracles. We have no desire that the work in which we are engaged should be considered an extraordinary, or even a remarkable one. We are truly sorry that many persons, inconsiderately, look upon it as almost miraculous.

The principles are as old as the Holy Scriptures. But they are forgotten by many; are not held in living faith by others; and by some they are not known at all; nay, they are denied to be Scriptural by not a few, and are considered wild and fanatical.

My success is ascribed to being a *foreigner* by birth, or to the *novelty* of the thing, or to some *secret treasure* to which I have access; but when all will not account for the progress of the work, it is said, the reports produce it all.

My reply is, that being a *foreigner*, by birth, would be much more likely to hinder my being entrusted with large sums, than to induce donors to give; and as to *novelty* procuring the money, the time is long gone by for novelty, for the institution has now been forty years in existence.

As to the *secret treasure* that I have access to, there is more in this supposition than those who say so are aware of; for surely God's treasury is inexhaustible, and I have drawn out of it, simply by prayer and faith, more than six hundred thousand pounds.

But now as to the statement that it is simply the reports which bring in the money, my reply is: there is nothing unusual in writing reports. This is done by public institutions generally; but the constant complaint is, that reports are not read. Our reports are not extraordinary as to power of language, or striking appeals. They are simple statements of facts. They are sent to donors, or to any individuals who wish to purchase them. If they produce results, which reports generally do not, I can only ascribe it to the Lord.

I do not mean to say that God does not use the reports as instruments in procuring means. They are written in order that I may give an account of my stewardship, and bring before the reader the operations of the institution; but particularly in order that, by these printed accounts, the chief end of this institution may be answered, which is to raise a public testimony to an unbelieving world that, in these last days, God is still the Living God . . . But while these are the *primary* reasons for publishing these reports, we doubt not that the Lord has again and again used them as instruments in leading persons to help us.

6

In Every Believer

How to live like Müller

'Make but trial'

Müller insisted, as we have seen (page 31), that he had not received a special gift of faith. It followed that there was no reason why every Christian should not enjoy a victorious life of faith. This extract is from part 3 of Müller's *Narratives*, first published in 1845.

I beseech you, do not think me an extraordinary believer, having privileges above other of God's dear children which they cannot have; nor look on my way of acting as something that would not do for other believers.

Make but trial! Do but stand still in the hour of trial, and you will see the help of God if you trust in Him. But there is so often a forsaking the ways of the Lord in the hour of trial, and thus the *food of faith*, the means whereby our faith may be increased, is lost. This leads me to the following important point. You ask, How may I, a true believer, have my faith strengthened?

How our faith may be strengthened

The answer is this:

I. 'Every good and perfect gift is from above, coming down from the Father of the heavenly lights, Who does not change like shifting shadows.' James 1:17. As the increase of faith is a good gift, it must come from God, and therefore He ought to be asked for this blessing.

II. The following means however ought to be used:

1. *The careful reading of the Word of God, combined with meditation on it*. Through reading the Word of God, and especially through meditation on the Word of God, the believer becomes more and more acquainted with the nature and character of God, and thus sees more and more, besides

His holiness and justice, what a kind, loving, gracious, merciful, mighty, wise, and faithful Being He is, and therefore in poverty, affliction of body, bereavement in his family, difficulty in his service, want of a situation or employment, he will repose upon the *ability* of God to help him, because he has not only learned from His word that He is of almighty power and infinite wisdom, but he has also seen instance upon instance in the Holy Scriptures in which His almighty power and infinite wisdom have been actually exercised in helping and delivering His people; and he will repose upon the *willingness* of God to help him, because he has not only learned from the Scriptures what a kind, good, merciful, gracious, and faithful Being God is, but because he has also seen in the Word of God, how in a great variety of instances He has proved Himself to be so. And the consideration of this, if *God has become known to us through prayer and meditation on His own Word*, will lead us, in general at least, with a measure of confidence to rely upon Him.

2. As with reference to the growth of every grace of the Spirit it is of the utmost importance that we seek to maintain an upright heart and a good conscience, and therefore do not knowingly and habitually indulge in those things which are contrary to the mind of God, so it is also particularly the case with reference to the *growth in faith*. How can I possibly continue to act in faith upon God, concerning anything, if I am habitually grieving Him, and seek to detract from the glory and honour of Him in whom I profess to trust, upon whom I profess to depend?

All my confidence towards God, all my leaning upon Him in the hour of trial will be gone, if I have a guilty conscience, and do not seek to put away this guilty conscience, but still continue to do things which are contrary to the mind of God. And if, in any particular instance, I cannot trust in God, because of the guilty conscience, then my faith is weakened by that instance of distrust; for faith with every trial of it either increases by trusting God, and thus getting help, or it decreases by not trusting Him; and then there is less and less power of looking simply and directly to Him, and a habit of self-dependence is begotten or encouraged.

3. If we desire our faith to be strengthened we should not shrink from opportunities where our faith may be tried, and

therefore, through the trial, be strengthened. In our natural state we dislike dealing with God alone. Through our natural alienation from God we shrink from Him, and from eternal realities. This cleaves to us more or less, even after our regeneration. Hence it is that, more or less, even as believers, we have the same shrinking from standing with God alone, from depending on Him alone, from looking to Him alone; and yet this is the very position in which we ought to be, if we wish our faith to be strengthened.

The more I am in a position to be tried in faith with reference to my body, my family, my service for the Lord, my business etc., the more shall I have opportunity of seeing God's help and deliverance; and every fresh instance in which He helps and delivers me will tend towards the increase of my faith.

4. The last important point for the strengthening of our faith is: that we let God work for us, when the hour of the trial of our faith comes, and do not work a deliverance of our own. Wherever God has given faith, it is given, among other reasons, for the very purpose of being tried. However weak our faith may be, God will try it; only with this restriction, that as in every way he leads on gently, gradually, patiently, so also with reference to the trial of our faith. At first our faith will be tried very little in comparison with what it may be afterwards; for God never lays more upon us than He is willing to enable us to bear.

Now when the trial of faith comes, we are naturally inclined to distrust God, and to trust rather in ourselves, or in our friends, or in our circumstances. We will rather work a deliverance of our own somehow or other, than simply look to God and wait for His help. But if we do not patiently wait for God's help, if we work a deliverance of our own, then at the next trial of our faith it will be thus again, and we shall be again inclined to deliver ourselves.

Would the believer therefore have his faith strengthened, he must especially *give time to God*, who tries his faith in order to prove to His child, in the end, how willing He is to help and deliver him the moment it is good for him.

Dr Sawtell's visit and the growth of faith

The Reverend Dr Sawtell was chaplain to British and American seamen at Le Havre. In March, 1860, he visited Müller's children's homes on Ashley Down, and these extracts are from a letter he wrote to the Reverend Francis Wayland later that year.

For the last five years my duties have called me frequently to England, Scotland, and Ireland, but I do not remember making one of these preaching tours without hearing more or less of what many called 'a standing miracle at Bristol' – *a man sheltering, feeding, clothing, educating, and making comfortable and happy hundreds of poor orphan children, with no funds of his own, and no possible means of sustenance, save that which God sent him in answer to prayer.* Of course, such facts, coming from undoubted authority, and oft repeated, could not fail to arrest my attention, and cause me to ponder deeply these things in my heart; and every new fact that came to my ears served only to increase my irrepressible desire to 'turn aside and see this great sight'.

I confess, on my first visit in March, 1860, I had reserved to myself a wide margin for deductions and disappointment; but, after a few days of careful investigation, I left Bristol exclaiming, with the Queen of Sheba, 'The half had not been told me.'

Here I saw, indeed, seven hundred orphan children fed and provided for, by the hand of God, in answer to prayer, as literally and truly as Elijah was fed by ravens with meat which the Lord provided. And now, after an absence of nine months, I am here again, moving about among these seven hundred children, examining their writing, and the progress they have made in the various branches of study, and their different kinds of work, listening to their sweet voices in songs of praise to the God of the orphan, passing through all parts of these vast buildings that have been erected for their accommodation, conducting their family worship, and addressing four hundred of them at once, and three hundred at another, assembled in their respective dining-halls, the most silent, attentive, and earnest listeners I have ever addressed; then enjoying hours of sweet converse and prayer with Mr Müller himself – a privilege for which I shall ever thank God. O, it is good to be here!

But to the orphan-houses themselves. These are all built of stone, in the most complete and thorough manner. No pains have been spared in rendering them convenient, comfortable, and safe for children, and with special reference to warmth, light, ventilation, and cleanliness; and while all is in good taste, and exceedingly chaste and neat, it is all plain – nothing for show or ornament . . .

In appearance Mr Müller is tall, rather slender, standing six feet in his boots, and of a remarkably fine figure, with a grave German face, and dark-brownish eyes that kindle into a pleasing benevolent expression in conversation. His dress is the very same in cut and colour that he wore in the German university (his coat a long-tail frock), all in black, except the snow-white neck-tie, fastened with a common plain pin in front, the ends hid beneath a waistcoat buttoned up so high as to hide everything but the cravat; making his whole general appearance, whether in the pulpit or in the street, a perfect model of neatness and order. His hair is rather coarse, and black as jet . . .

Being seated with Mr Müller at his own table, a few evenings since, the subject of faith naturally became the topic of conversation, when he beautifully remarked, 'The first germ of faith in the soul is very much like a new-born infant in the cradle, very small and very weak, and its future growth and increase of strength as much depend on its daily, constant exercise, as does the physical development of the child; yes,' continued he, 'I can now as easily trust God for thirty-five thousand pounds as I could at first for five thousand.'

Now, may not Mr Müller's experience on this vital and fundamental principle of our holy religion reveal to us the secret cause of our own weak faith? We fold it up, as it were, in a napkin, lay it carefully away, and treat it as a tender but foolish mother does her offspring: afraid of the open air, it will take cold; it must not walk out, it will fall and break its limbs; it must not take nutritious food, it is so delicate. Thus the poor, unfortunate child never rises to the full strength and vigour of manhood.

So is it with that class of believers who do little else than to nurse and sing a kind of lullaby over their puny faith; it must never venture out of sight, or upon a stormy sea in a dark night, or, in other words, *never trust God*. O, what a misnomer to call this faith! and what is it worth, even if it can be called faith? So far as the wants of this perishing world are concerned, it is as worthless as the one talent buried in the earth, and if sufficient to save the soul, it can be saved 'only as by fire'. Let us not fail here to mark well the difference between these two grains of faith, both small and weak at the beginning, but one by daily vigorous exercise increases and grows into such mighty strength 'that as a prince it hath power with God', while the other, for want of exercise, sinks into imbecility, and becomes powerless for good.

Coping with difficulties

Müller opened the fifth and last of his children's homes on Ashley Down in January, 1870. The extract which follows is his description of how, in 1864, he acquired the eighteen-acre site on which he built the last two homes. He recorded the saga of events in some detail so that the reader, in his words, 'may not be discouraged by difficulties, however great and many and varied, but give himself to prayer, trusting in the Lord for help'. The passage demonstrates Müller's typical combination of prayer with shrewd business sense.

My eyes had been for years directed to a beautiful piece of land, only separated by the turnpike road from the ground on which the new orphan-house number three is erected. The land is about eighteen acres, with a small house and out-houses built on one end thereof. Hundreds of times had I prayed, within the last years, that God for Jesus' sake would count me worthy to be allowed to erect on this ground two more orphan-houses; and hundreds of times I had with a prayerful eye looked on this land, yea, as it were, bedewed it with my prayers.

I might have bought it years ago; but that would have been going before the Lord. I had money enough in hand to have paid for it years ago; but I desired patiently, submissively, to wait God's own time and for Him to mark it clearly and distinctly that His time was come, and that I took the step according to His will; for whatever I might apparently accomplish, if the work were mine, and not the Lord's, I could expect no blessing. But now the Lord's mind was clearly and distinctly made manifest. I had enough money in hand to pay for the land and to build one house, and therefore I went forward, after having still asked the Lord for guidance, and being assured that it was His will I should take active steps.

The first thing I did was to see the agent who acted for the owner of the land to ask him whether the land was for sale. He replied that it was, but that it was let till March 25, 1867. He said that he would write for the price. Here a great difficulty at once presented itself, that the land was let for two years and four months longer, whilst it appeared desirable that I should be able to take possession of it in about six months, that is, as soon as the conveyance could be made out, and the plans be ready for the new orphan house number four, and arrangements be made with contractors.

But I was not discouraged by this difficulty; for I expected through prayer to make happy and satisfactory arrangements with the tenant, being willing to give him fair compensation for leaving before his time had expired. But, before I had time to see about this, two other great difficulties presented themselves: the one was that the owner asked seven thousand pounds for the land, which I judged to be considerably more than its value; and the other, that I heard that the Bristol Waterworks Company intended to make an additional reservoir for their water on this very land, and to get an Act of Parliament passed to that effect.

Pause here for a few moments, esteemed reader. You have seen how the Lord brought me so far with regard to pecuniary means that I now felt warranted to go forward; and I may further add that I was brought to this point as the result of thousands of times praying regarding this object; and that there were also many hundreds of children waiting for admission; and yet, after the Lord Himself so manifestly had appeared on our behalf, by the donation of five thousand pounds [on November 3, 1864], He allows this apparent death-blow to come upon the whole.

But thus I have found it hundreds of times since I have known the Lord. The difficulties which He is pleased to allow to arise are only allowed under such circumstances for the exercise of our faith and patience; and more prayer, more patience, and the exercise of faith, will remove the difficulties.

Now, as I knew the Lord, these difficulties were no insurmountable difficulties to me, for I put my trust in Him, according to that word: 'The Lord also will be a refuge for the oppressed, a refuge in times of trouble. And they that know Your name will put their trust in You: for You, Lord, have not forsaken those that seek You' Psalm 9:9–10. I gave myself therefore earnestly to prayer concerning all these three especial difficulties which had arisen regarding the land. I prayed several times daily about the matter, and used the following means.

1. I saw the Acting Committee of the Directors of the Bristol Waterworks Company regarding their intended reservoir on the land which I was about to purchase, and stated to them what I had seen in print concerning their intentions. They courteously stated to me that only a small portion of the land would be required, not enough to interfere with my purpose; and that, if it could be avoided, even this small portion should not be taken.

2. This being settled, I now saw the tenant, after many prayers; for I desired, as a Christian, that if this land were bought, it should be done under amicable circumstances with regard to him. At the first interview, I stated my intentions to him, at the same time expressing my desire that the matter should be settled pleasantly with regard to himself. He said that he would consider the matter, and desired a few days for that purpose. After a week I saw him again, and he then kindly stated that, as the land was wanted for such an object, he would not stand in the way; but that, as he had laid out a good deal on the house and land, he expected a compensation for leaving it before his time was up. As I, of course, was quite willing to give a *fair* and *reasonable* compensation, I considered this a very precious answer to prayer.

3. I now entered upon the third difficulty, the price of the land. I knew well how much the land was worth to the orphan institution; but its value to the institution was not the market

value. I gave myself therefore day by day to prayer that the Lord would constrain the owner to accept a considerably lower sum than he had asked; I also pointed out to him why it was not worth as much as he asked.

At last he consented to take five thousand five hundred instead of seven thousand pounds, and I accepted the offer; for I knew that by the level character of the land we should save a considerable sum for the two houses, and that by the new sewer, which only a few months before had been completed, running along under the turnpike road near the field, we should be considerably benefited. In addition to these two points I had to take into the account that we can have gas from Bristol, as in the three houses already in operation. And lastly, the most important point of all, the nearness of this piece of land to the other three houses, so that all could easily be under the same direction and superintendence. In fact, no other piece of land, near or far off, would present so much advantage to us as this spot, which the Lord thus so very kindly had given to us. All being now settled, I proceeded to have the land conveyed to the same trustees who stood trustees for the new orphan houses number one, number two, and number three.

I have thus minutely dwelt on these various matters for the encouragement of the reader, that he may not be discouraged by difficulties, however great and many and varied, but give himself to prayer, trusting in the Lord for help, yea, expecting help, which, in His own time and way, He will surely grant.

Believing God's promises

When he was seventy-five, Müller preached a major sermon on prayer. He began by reading two of the verses which had meant so much to him half a century earlier when he had decided to abandon any idea of salary (page 22): 'Ask and it shall be given to you; seek and you will find; knock and the door will be opened to you. For everyone who asks receives; he who seeks finds; and to him who knocks, the door will be opened' (Matt. 7:7–8). Then he said:

Our Heavenly Father loves all His children with infinite love; that is, He loves every one, even the feeblest and weakest of His children with the self-same love with which He loves His only begotten Son. On account of this infinite love – knowing how great, how many, how varied, nay, how numberless would be their trials, their difficulties, their afflictions, their temptations, while passing through this vale of tears – He, in His grace, made abundant provision, in giving most precious and encouraging promises concerning prayer: so that if they would take their trials, difficulties, afflictions and temptations to their Heavenly Father, seeking His strength, His counsel, and His guidance, and acting according to the loving counsel and advice given in the Scriptures – 'Casting all your care upon Him' – the position of most of the children of God would be very different from what it is.

Then again, our precious Lord Jesus Christ loves us with the self-same love with which the Father loves Him. Do we all believe it?

It may appear strange to some of you that the Father loves His children with the self-same love with which He loves His only begotten Son, and that the Lord Jesus Christ loves us with that same love – and that with this love He loves the feeblest and weakest of His children. Yet this is the statement found in the Bible at John 15:9 and 17:23. Our precious Lord Jesus Christ who loves us with such love, passed through difficulties, trials, and temptations, like unto ours, while He was in this world. He was looked down upon; He was despised; that Blessed One 'had not where to lay His head'; and was, while in this world 'in all points tempted like as we are, yet without sin'.

Knowing the position of His disciples in this world, He has given the precious promise which I have read on the subject of prayer, and if it is made good of, we may have Him as the burden-bearer, ever ready to help in time of sorrow, weakness and affliction – in a word, in all the variety of positions and circumstances in which we are found here in the body.

Had it been left to us to make promises regarding prayer, I do not know that you or I could have done more than say, 'Ask, and you shall receive.' Yet while the promise is so full, so deep, so broad, so precious in every way, we have here – as becomes us with other parts of the Word of God – to compare

Scripture with Scripture, because in other parts additions are made, or conditions given, which if we neglect will hinder our getting the full benefit of prayer.

The conditions of successful prayer

Müller continued his sermon:

I judge we have not to lose sight of the passage in 1 John 5:13–15, especially the words, 'If we ask anything according to His will He hears us, and if we know that He hears us, whatever we ask, we know that we have the petitions that we desired of Him.'

Here then is the first point to be noticed with regard to prayer. If we desire to have our petitions granted, it becomes us first to see to it that we ask for things according to His mind and will; for our blessing and happiness are intimately connected with the holiness of God.

Suppose there were living in Bristol a person who had long carried on a business, who was known by those intimately acquainted with him to be an idle person, one who shrinks from work; or, whenever he can, gets out of it, and seeks to have an easy time of it. Suppose such a person had heard the promises about prayer, and should say, 'Now I will try if these things are true, and I will ask God to give me a hundred thousand pounds sterling, and then I can give myself easy days; I can travel about and enjoy myself.' Suppose he prays every day for this large sum of money, will he obtain it? Assuredly not! Why not? He does not ask for it that he may help the poor abundantly; that he may contribute to the work of God more liberally, but he asks that he may spend his life in idleness, and in enjoying the pleasures of the world. He is not asking for things according to the mind of God, and therefore however long or earnestly he may pray, he will not get the answer. We are only warranted in expecting our prayers to be answered when we ask for things according to the mind of God.

The second point we should notice is, that we do not ask on account of our own goodness or merit, but, as the Scripture expresses it, 'In the name of the Lord Jesus Christ.' I refer you to John 14: 13-14: 'And whatever you shall ask in My name, that will I do, that the Father may be glorified in the Son. If you shall ask anything in My name, I will do it.' The statement is given twice, in order to show the great importance of the truth.

What does this statement, given twice by the Lord Jesus Christ, mean? It means that just as by faith in the Lord Jesus Christ we shall stand before God at the last, so it is now in approaching unto God in prayer. If we desire to have our petitions answered, we must come to Him, not in our own name, but as sinners who trust in Jesus, who by faith in His name are united to the blessed risen Lord, who have become, through trusting in Him, members of that body of which He is the head.

Let none suppose they are good enough in themselves. I deserve nothing but hell. For fifty-four years and nine months, by God's grace, I have walked in the fear of God, and by His grace have lived such a life that no one can point to me and say I am a hypocrite, or charge me with living in any sin. Yet if I had what I deserve, I could expect nothing but hell. I deserve nothing but hell. So precisely with all of you, and the very best and holiest persons that can be found.

Therefore on the ground of our goodness we cannot expect to have our prayers answered. But Jesus is worthy, and for His sake we may have our prayers answered. There is nothing too choice, too costly, or too great for God to give to Him. He is worthy. He is the spotless, holy child, who under all circumstances acted according to the mind of God. And if we trust in Him, if we hide in Him, if we put Him forward, and ourselves in the background, depend on Him and plead His name, we may expect to have our prayers answered.

Someone may say, 'I have prayed through long years for my unconverted children, but they have not yet been converted. I feel I shall not have my prayers answered. I am so unworthy.' This is a mistake. The promises are particularly for such – for the weak, for the feeblest, for the ignorant, for the needy; and all such who ask for Christ's sake are warranted to expect their prayers to be answered.

But if it mean, 'I live in sin, I go on habitually in an evil course,' the prayer cannot be answered, for in the sixty-sixth

Psalm we read, 'If I regard iniquity in my heart, the Lord will not hear me.' That is, if I live in sin, and go on in a course hateful to God, I may not expect my prayers to be answered.

A third condition is that we exercise faith in the power and willingness of God to answer our prayers. This is deeply important. In Mark 11:24, we read, 'What things you desire, when you pray, believe that you receive them, and you shall have them.'

I have found invariably, in the fifty-four years and nine months during which I have been a believer, that if I only believed I was sure to get, in God's time, the thing I asked for. I would especially lay this on your heart that you exercise faith in the power and willingness of God to answer your requests. We must believe that God is able and willing. To see that He is able, you only have to look at the resurrection of the Lord Jesus Christ; for having raised Him from the dead, He must have almighty power. As to the love of God, you have only to look to the cross of Christ, and see His love in not sparing His son from death. With these proofs of the power and love of God, assuredly, if we believe, we shall receive – we shall obtain.

Suppose now we ask, firstly, for such things as are according to the mind of God, and only such things as are good for us; secondly, that we expect answers on the ground of the merit and righteousness of the Lord Jesus Christ, asking in His name; and thirdly, that we exercise faith in the power and willingness of our Heavenly Father to grant our requests; then, fourthly, we have to continue patiently waiting on God till the blessing we seek is granted.

For observe, nothing is said in the text as to the time in which, or the circumstances under which, the prayer is to be answered. 'Ask, and it shall be given you.' There is a positive promise, but nothing as to the time. 'Seek, and you shall find; knock, and it shall be opened unto you.' We have therefore patiently and quietly to continue waiting on God till the blessing is granted.

Why prayer may not be answered immediately

Müller continued:

Someone may say, 'Is it necessary I should bring a matter before God two, three, five, or even twenty times; is it not enough I tell Him once?' We might as well say there is no need to tell Him once, for He knows beforehand what our need is. He wants us to prove that we have confidence in Him, that we take our place as creatures towards the Creator.

Moreover we are never to lose sight of the fact that there may be particular reasons why prayer may not at once be answered. One reason may be the need for the exercise of our faith, for by exercise faith is strengthened. We all know that if our faith were not exercised it would remain as it was at first. By the trial it is strengthened. Another reason may be that we may glorify God by the manifestation of patience. This is a grace by which God is greatly magnified. Our manifestation of patience glorifies God. There may be another reason. Our heart may not yet be prepared for the answer to our prayer.

I will give an illustration. Suppose that three weeks ago a lad of sixteen years of age had been brought to the knowledge of the Lord Jesus Christ, and that with his heart full of love to the Lord he wanted to do something for the Lord. And suppose he goes to the superintendent of the Sunday School, and says, 'Will you have the kindness to give me a class to teach?'

A class of nine children is given to him. Now this dear lad, whose heart is full of love to the Lord, begins to pray that God would convert these nine children. He prays in private and before them, and also exhorts them to seek the Lord. After going home from his class he gives himself earnestly to prayer that God would convert these nine children. On Monday he repeats his request before God, and so day by day during the week and on Sunday again particularly; and then he goes to his class and expects that these nine children will be converted.

He finds however that they are not, but that they are just in

the same state as before. He again sets the Gospel before
them; he exhorts, beseeches, and weeps before them. During
the second week his prayers are most earnest; but on the
following Sunday he finds that none of the nine children are
yet converted.

Does it mean that God will not answer these prayers? It
cannot be that this dear lad will have to go on praying, and
God not regard it. But the reason is that the heart of this lad is
not prepared for the blessing. If these children had been
converted the first week, he would take credit to himself; he
would think what he had been able to do, and would attribute
the conversions to his entreaties, instead of to the power of the
Holy Spirit. He would take a goodly measure of credit to
himself, though he might not be aware of it. But let him
patiently go on, and when his heart is prepared for the
blessing, God will give it.

Thus it is that the child of God has to wait; but when the
heart is prepared for the blessing, most assuredly it will be
given. Many of the dear children of God stagger, because
prayer is not at once answered. And because for weeks,
months, and years prayer remains unanswered, they cease to
ask God, and thus they lose the blessing which, had they
persevered, they would assuredly have obtained.

It should be especially noticed that all the children of God,
who walk in His ways and wait on Him in prayer, have, more
or less frequently, answers to prayer. I will illustrate this. All
who in any measure walk before God, at the close of the day
thank Him for His mercies, and commend themselves to Him
for protection during the night. In the morning they find no
fire has happened and no wicked hands have molested them.
Here is an answer to prayer, and we have to thank God for it.
The more we observe these matters, the more we shall find
how we get prayer answered. Many that have suffered from
sleeplessness have often, in answer to prayer, had sound
refreshing sleep, and have had in the morning to thank God
for it.

Now all, on the other hand, have sometimes long to wait for
answers to prayer. Many of the dear children of God have
long to wait for the conversion of their children. While some
receive the blessing very soon, others have to wait for many
years. I have had immediate answers to prayer, so that I could

reckon them by tens of thousands. If I say that during the fifty-four years and nine months that I have been a believer in the Lord Jesus Christ I have had thirty thousand answers to prayer, either in the same hour or the same day that the requests were made, I should not go a particle too far. Often, before leaving my bedroom in the morning, have I had prayer answered that was offered that morning, and in the course of the day I have had five or six more answers to prayer; so that at least thirty thousand prayers have been answered the self-same hour or the self-same day that they were offered.

But one or the other might suppose all my prayers have been thus promptly answered. No; not all of them. Sometimes I have had to wait weeks, months, or years; sometimes many years. The man speaking at the present time, whom God has delighted to honour by giving thirty thousand answers to prayer in the same hour or day on which they were offered, this self-same man has had to wait many years for answers to many of his prayers.

I asked once a thing of God, which I knew to be according to His mind, and though I brought it day by day and generally many times a day before Him, in such assurance as to be able to thank Him hundreds of times for the answer before it was received, yet I had to wait three years and ten months before the blessing was given to me. At another time I had to wait six years; and at another time eleven and a half years. In the last case I brought the matter about twenty thousand times before God, and invariably in the fullest assurance of faith, and yet eleven and a half years passed before the answer was given.

In one instance my faith has been tried even more than this. In November, 1844, I began to pray for the conversion of five individuals. I prayed every day without one single intermission, whether sick or in health, on the land or on the sea, and whatever the pressure of my engagements might be. Eighteen months elapsed before the first of the five was converted. I thanked God, and prayed on for the others. Five years elapsed, and then the second was converted. I thanked God for the second, and prayed on for the other three. Day by day I continued to pray for them, and six years more passed before the third was converted. I thanked God for the three, and went on praying for the other two. These two remain unconverted. The man to whom God in the riches of his grace has given tens of thousands of answers to prayer, in the self-same hour or day on which they were offered, has been praying day by day for nearly thirty-six years for the conversion of these two individuals, and yet they remain unconverted; for next November it will be thirty-six years since I began to pray for their conversion. But I hope in God, I pray on and look yet for the answer.

Therefore, beloved brethren and sisters, go on waiting upon God, go on praying; only be sure you ask for things which are according to the mind of God. The conversion of sinners is according to the mind of God, for He does not desire the death of a sinner. Go on praying; expect an answer, look for it, and in the end you will have to praise God for it.

There is one point I would especially lay on the hearts of my beloved brethren and sisters, and that is – united prayer. In Matthew 18:19, the Lord Jesus says, 'If two of you shall agree on earth as touching anything that they shall ask, it shall be done for them of my Father which is in Heaven.'

If therefore there are brethren and sisters in Christ who have unconverted relatives, and if they could unite with two or more persons, and unitedly ask God to convert their children, oh, what blessing might not come in this way? They should plead this promise before the Lord, read it out when they meet, and put their finger – so to speak – upon it. If they meet once a week for a half an hour, or once a fortnight, or as often as they conveniently could, to plead this promise before the Lord, after a while a father would have to say, 'My son, who almost broke my heart, has been converted,' and a mother, 'I have a letter from my daughter, who fifteen years ago left my home, and has been living in sin, telling me she has found the Lord Jesus Christ.'

How their faith would be strengthened by such united prayer and such testimonies! After a while, as their faith got strengthened, they would unitedly pray for their pastor, that God would more abundantly bless his labours in the conversion of sinners, and in blessing on the Church; and as they got further enlarged their prayers would extend to missions, the circulation of the Scriptures and tracts. They would know the power and blessedness of prayer more and more abundantly, and would wait earnestly upon God, asking him yet once more, in these days, to grant a mighty revival in the Church of Christ at large.

I have found it a great blessing to treasure up in the memory the answers God graciously gives me. I have always kept a record to strengthen the memory. I advise the keeping of a little memorandum book. On one side – say the left hand side – put down the petition and the date when you began to offer it. Let the opposite page be left blank to put down the answer in each case, and you will soon find how many answers you get, and thus you will be encouraged more and more, your faith will be strengthened; and especially you will see what a lovely, bountiful, and gracious Being God is; your heart will go out more and more in love to God, and you will say, 'It is my Heavenly Father who has been so kind, I will trust in Him, I will confide in Him.'

With regard to any who do not yet know Him, let the first prayer be offered tonight, before you leave this place – 'Show me I am a sinner'. When you see this, ask the Lord, 'Help me to put my trust in the Lord Jesus Christ,' and you will find how ready God is to give blessing. May we all who are the people of God receive a blessing, and our dear friends and fellow-sinners be stirred up to seek Him while He is to be found! God grant it for Jesus' sake.

One of the two men referred to by Müller in his sermon, for whom he had prayed for thirty-six years, was converted before Müller died and the other became a Christian after Müller's death.

Honey from the rock

In a widely circulated tract, Müller wrote:

'Open wide your mouth and I will fill it' (Psalm 81:10). This word should be continually present to our hearts. We all have our necessities of one kind or another, and every child of God has many things about which he has need to speak to God. And our gracious God speaks here to each one of His children: 'Open wide your mouth and I will fill it.' It is as if He said, 'Now ask much at My hands, look for much from

Me, bring great requests before Me. I am God, and not man; it is the very joy and delight of My heart to give abundantly.'

If we were privileged to go to a great person for anything, we should not ask for twopence-ha'penny, nor two shillings only, but much more; it would be an insult to ask for so little. And if we were allowed freely to make our requests before the Sovereign, we should be ashamed, or ought to be, to make only trifling requests. But the mighty ones of the earth are as nothing compared with Jehovah; and if we would give joy to the heart of God, we must ask great things at His hands, and expect great things from Him. This is taught us in the figurative expression, 'Open wide your mouth,' and the promise is, 'I will fill it.' Let anyone act according to that exhortation, and most assuredly God will fulfil the promise.

Let us look about, and see when in any measure we have been able to act according to this word, whether God was not as good as His word; let us remember that if He has not yet gratified our requests, it does not follow that He will not. Let us only wait still on Him expectingly, perseveringly, for the glory of God, in the name of Jesus, and we shall see how He will fulfil this word, 'I will fill it.'

How touching are those words in the same Psalm, where God says, 'If My people would but listen to Me, if Israel would follow My ways, how quickly would I subdue their enemies and turn My hand against their foes! Those who hate the Lord would cringe before Him, and their punishment would last for ever. But you would be fed with the finest of wheat; with honey from the rock I would satisfy you.' It is the very joy and delight of the heart of God to do us good; and we are here taught that God is willing to give us everything really good for us.

Christian giving 1:
Acting as stewards

This is an extract from Müller's journal for 1849.

August 30. Received a fifty pound note with these words: 'I send you herewith a fifty pound note, half for the missions, half for the orphans, unless you are in any personal need; if so, take five pounds for yourself. This will be the last large sum I shall be able to transmit to you. Almost all the rest is already out at interest.' I took half of this fifty pounds for the orphans and half for missionaries. The writer sold some time since his only earthly possession, and sent me at different times sums of a hundred and twenty pounds, of a hundred pounds, of fifty-five pounds, of fifty pounds and of twenty pounds for the work of the Lord in my hands. When he says therefore, 'The rest is already *out at interest*,' he means that he has given it away for the Lord, which indeed both for time and eternity is the very best way of using the means with which the Lord may be pleased to intrust us, in so far as, considering in the fear of God all our various claims and duties and relationships, we may do so.

In his *Narratives* Müller added the following comments.

As this is written for the spiritual profit of the reader, I cannot but add to this extract from my journal that since that time I have received other donations from the same donor, and much larger still. He used for God the means with which He was pleased to intrust him, and, contrary to this brother's expectation, the above fifty pounds was not the last large donation; for it pleased God soon after to intrust him with another considerable sum, which he again used for the Lord.

This did not at all surprise me; for it is the Lord's order, that, in whatever way He is pleased to make us His stewards, whether as to temporal or spiritual things, if we are indeed acting as *stewards* and not as *owners*, he will make us stewards over *more*.

Christian giving 2: Treasures in Heaven

This extract from Müller's *Narratives* may make you feel uncomfortable –unless you are in the habit, as Müller was, of taking all Christ's words seriously. The verses quoted are from our Lord's sermon on the mount.

In Matthew 6:19–21, we read: 'Do not store up for yourselves treasures on earth, where moth and rust destroy, and where thieves break in and steal. But store up for yourselves treasures in Heaven, where moth and rust do not destroy, and where thieves do not break in and steal. For where your treasure is, there your heart will be also.' Observe the following points concerning this part of the divine testimony.

1. It is the Lord Jesus, our Lord and Master, who speaks this as the lawgiver of His people. He who has infinite wisdom and unfathomable love to us, who therefore both knows what is for our real welfare and happiness, and who cannot exact from us any requirement inconsistent with that love which led Him to lay down His life for us. Remembering, then, who it is who speaks to us in these verses, let us consider them.

2. His counsel, His affectionate entreaty, and His commandment to us His disciples is: 'Do not store up for yourselves treasures on earth.' The meaning obviously is that the disciples of the Lord Jesus, being strangers and pilgrims on earth, i.e. neither belonging to the earth nor expecting to remain in it, *should not seek to increase their earthly possessions*, in whatever these possessions may consist.

This is a word for poor believers as well as rich believers; it has as much reference to putting shillings into the savings bank as to putting thousands of pounds into funds, or purchasing one house, or one farm after another.

It may be said: but does not every prudent and provident person seek to increase his means, that he may have a goodly portion to leave to his children, or to have something for old age, or for the time of sickness, etc.?

My reply is, it is quite true that this is the custom of the world. It was thus in the days of our Lord, and Paul refers to this custom of the world when he says, 'Children should not have to save up for their parents, but parents for their children' (2 Cor. 12:14). But whilst thus it is in the world, and we have every reason to believe ever will be so among those that are of the world, and who therefore have their portion on earth, we disciples of the Lord Jesus, being born again, being the children of God not nominally, but really, being truly partakers of the divine nature, being in fellowship with the Father and the Son, and having in prospect 'an inheritance that can never perish, spoil or fade' (1 Peter 1:4), ought in every respect to act differently from the world, and so in this particular also.

If we disciples of the Lord Jesus seek, like the people of the world, after an increase of our possessions, may not those who are of the world justly question whether we believe what we say when we speak about our inheritance, our heavenly calling, our being the children of God, and so on? Often it must be a sad stumbling block to the unbeliever to see a professed believer in the Lord Jesus acting in this particular just like himself. Consider this, dear brethren in the Lord, should this remark apply to you.

I have more than once had the following passage quoted to me as a proof that parents ought to lay up money for their children, or husbands for their wives: 'If anyone does not provide for his relatives, and especially for his immediate family, he has denied the faith and is worse than an unbeliever' (1 Tim. 5:8). It is however concerning this verse only needful, in childlike simplicity, to read the connexion from verse three to five, and it will be obvious that the meaning is this, that whilst the poor widows of the Church are to be cared for by the Church, yet if any such needy believing widow had children or grandchildren (not nephews), these children or grandchildren should provide for the widow, that the Church might not be charged; but that if a believer's child or grandchild in such a case did not do so, such a one did not act according to the obligations laid upon him by his holy faith, and was worse than an unbeliever. Not a word then is there in this passage to favour the laying up of treasures upon earth for our children or our wives.

3. Our Lord says concerning the earth that it is a place 'where moth and rust destroy, and where thieves break in and steal'. All that is of the earth, and in any way connected with it, is subject to corruption, to change, to dissolution. There is no reality, or substance, in anything else but in heavenly things. Often the careful amassing of earthly possessions ends in losing them in a moment of fire, by robbery, by a change of mercantile concerns, by loss of work, and so on; but suppose all this were not the case, still yet a little while, and your soul shall be required of you; or, yet a little while, and the Lord Jesus will return; and what profit shall you have, dear reader, if you have carefully sought to increase your earthly

possessions? My brother, if there were one particle of real benefit to be derived from it, would not He, whose love to us has been proved to the uttermost, have wished that you and I should have it? If, in the least degree, it could tend to the increase of our peace, or joy in the Holy Spirit, or heavenly-mindedness, He, who laid down His life for us, would have commanded us to '*store up* treasures on earth'.

4. Our Lord however does not merely bid us *not* to store up treasures on earth; for if He had said no more, this His commandment might be abused, and persons might find in it an encouragement for their extravagant habits, for their love of pleasure, for their habit of spending everything they have, or can obtain, *upon themselves*. It does not mean, then, as is the common phrase, that we should 'live up to our income'; for He adds: 'but store up for yourselves treasures in Heaven'.

There is such a thing as storing up as truly in Heaven as there is storing up on earth; if it were not so, our Lord would not have said so. Just as persons put one sum after another into the bank, and it is put down to their credit, and they may use the money afterwards: so truly the penny, the pound, the hundred pounds, the ten thousand pounds, *given for the Lord's sake, and constrained by the love of Jesus,* to poor brethren, or in any way spent in the work of God, He marks down in the book of remembrance, He considers as laid up in Heaven. *The money is not lost, it is laid up in the bank of Heaven*; yet so, that, whilst an earthly bank may break, or through earthly circumstances we may lose our earthly possessions, the money which is thus secured in Heaven *cannot be lost*.

But this is by no means the only difference. I notice a few more points.

Treasures stored up on earth bring along with them many cares; treasures stored up in Heaven never give care.

Treasures stored up on earth never can afford spiritual joy; treasures stored up in Heaven bring along with them peace and joy in the Holy Spirit even now.

Treasures stored up on earth in a dying hour cannot afford peace and comfort, and when life is over they are taken from us; treasures stored up in Heaven draw forth thanksgiving that we were permitted and counted worthy to serve the Lord with means with which He was pleased to intrust us as stewards.

And when this life is over we are not deprived of what was stored up there, but when we go to Heaven we go to the place where our treasures are, and we shall find them there.

Often we hear it said when a person has died: he died worth so much. But whatever be the phrases common in the world, it is certain that a person may die worth fifty thousand pounds sterling, as the world reckons, and yet that individual may not possess in the sight of God one thousand pounds sterling, because *he was not rich towards God*, he did not store up treasure in Heaven. And so, on the other hand, we can suppose a man of God falling asleep in Jesus, and his surviving widow finding scarcely enough left behind him to suffice for the funeral, who was nevertheless *rich towards God*; in the sight of God he may possess five thousand pounds sterling, he may have laid up that sum in Heaven.

Does your soul long to be rich towards God, to store up treasures in Heaven? The world and its desires pass away (1 John 2:17)! Yet a little while and our stewardship will be taken from us. At present we have the opportunity of serving the Lord with our time, our talents, our bodily strength, our gifts, and also with our property; but shortly this opportunity may cease. Oh! how shortly may it cease. Before ever this is read by anyone I may have fallen asleep; and the very next day after you read this, dear reader, you may fall asleep, and therefore, whilst we have the opportunity, let us serve the Lord.

Suppose, after a little while, you should fall asleep, someone may say, Your wife and child will be unprovided for, because you did not make a provision for them. My reply is, The Lord will take care of them. The Lord will abundantly provide for them, as He now abundantly provides for us.

5. The Lord lastly adds: 'For where your treasure is, there your heart will be also.' Where should the heart of the disciple of the Lord Jesus be, but in Heaven? Our calling is a heavenly calling, our inheritance is a heavenly inheritance, and reserved for us in Heaven; our citizenship is in Heaven; but if we believers in the Lord Jesus store up treasures on earth, the necessary result of it is that our hearts will be upon earth; nay, the very fact of our doing so proves that we are there! Nor will it be otherwise till there be a ceasing to store up treasures

upon earth.

The believer who stores up treasures upon earth may at first not live openly in sin; he in a measure may yet bring some honour to the Lord in certain things; but the injurious tendencies of this habit will show themselves more and more, whilst the habit of storing up treasures in Heaven would draw the heart more and more heavenward; would be continually strengthening his new, his divine nature, his spiritual faculties, because it would call his spiritual faculties into use, and thus they would be strengthened; and he would more and more, whilst yet in the body, have his heart in Heaven, and set upon heavenly things; and thus the storing up treasures in Heaven would bring along with it, even in this life, precious spiritual blessings as a reward of obedience to the commandment of our Lord.

Christian giving 3: Cheerfully and systematically

During the course of an address at a Mildmay Park Conference in 1880, Müller said:

I have been for fifty years, by God's grace, acting on the principle of Christian giving according to the Scriptures, and I cannot tell you the abundance of spiritual blessing I have received to my own soul through acting thus; that is, seeking to be a cheerful giver; seeking to give as God has been pleased to prosper me.

I began when I had comparatively very little to spare; but as I gave, God increased my ability to give more and more: until at last God has been pleased in the riches of His grace, to condescend to use a poor worthless worm like me, and has entrusted me year by year with very large sums to expend.

Many beloved saints are depriving themselves of wondrous spiritual blessing by not giving as stewards what is entrusted to them. They act as if it were their own, as if all belonged to them, as if already they were in possession of the inheritance incorruptible and undefiled; forgetting that they have nothing whatever which is their own, that they are bought by the precious blood of Christ, and all they possess – their bodily strength, their time, their talents, their business, their professions, their eyes, their hands, their feet, all belong to the Lord Jesus Christ; because He has bought them with His precious blood.

Therefore may I affectionately beseech and entreat my beloved Christian friends to take this to heart, and consider that hitherto they have been depriving themselves of vast spiritual blessings, because they have not followed the principles of giving systematically, and giving as God prospers them, and according to a plan; not merely just according to impulse, not as they are moved by a missionary or charity sermon, but systematically and habitually giving on principle, just as God enables them. If he entrusts to them one pound, to give accordingly a proportion; if they are left a legacy of a thousand pounds, to give accordingly; if he entrusts them with ten thousand pounds, or whatever it may be, to give accordingly. Oh, my brethren, I believe if we realised the blessing, we would give thus on principle; and, if so, we should give a hundred times more than we do now.

Just as we are constrained by the love of Christ, so God condescends to use us; and as we give, He is pleased to entrust to us more and more. It is impossible for us to say to what amount God may entrust us, or how largely He may give unto us the joy and honour, the precious privilege, of communicating to others.

And here allow me to refer to my own experience. The first year I began giving God entrusted me with about fifty pounds; but this afterwards increased, until now he has entrusted me with about two thousand pounds a year. The poor man George Müller, known by everybody as a poor man, who stands before you a poor man, and yet by the grace of God has been enabled to give about forty thousand pounds sterling – that is altogether since I began.

Of late, God has allowed me to receive one legacy after another, and thus sometimes two thousand and even three thousand a year have I been enabled to give; and see the blessedness, the privilege, the wondrous honour, that a poor man as I am should thus be entrusted by Him!

By the grace of God I desire to be nothing but poor. I wish to be nothing else than a poor man, having nothing, no house of my own, no money in the funds, not an acre of land – a poor man altogether; day by day waiting on God for all I need, for the very clothes that I wear. I wait on God for everything.

Now why do I say all this? To encourage the hearts of my beloved brethren to seek to give systematically. If you have not done so hitherto, do begin now. It is a blessed thing for the soul, it is a blessed thing for your purse, and God will entrust to you more and more.

Now I do not say imitate me, George Müller; but I say, seek to give, if it be ever so little, to give systematically, and you will find a blessing to your soul; and the blessing with regard to stewardship will be such that you will be encouraged more and more to go on in this way.

Müller lived for another seventeen years after delivering this address and it is known that during the whole of his long life he received about ninety-three thousand pounds for his personal use. Of this he gave away over eighty-one thousand pounds and at his death his total estate was valued at about a hundred and sixty pounds, including household furniture.

In the final volume of his *Narratives*, published in 1886, Müller addressed himself to the question, 'How much shall I give of what I receive?'

The answer is, the Holy Scriptures of the New Testament lay down no rule. It is left to the children of God to act according to the measure of knowledge and grace they have received. The appreciation of what God has done for them in Christ should guide them. We have however not to lose sight of this, that if the Israelite was commanded to give the tenth of all he received, and that the Israelite, in addition to this, had *many* other expenses in connection with his being a worshipper of the True and Living God, such as the not sowing the seventh year, the going three times a year to the Lord's Tabernacle or Temple, and so on; the believer in the Lord Jesus – who knows the power of His precious blood, shed for the remission of his sins, who has the whole revealed will of God in his hands, who has received the Holy Spirit and who is a partaker of the heavenly calling – should certainly not do less than the Israelite.

We should not say that because we are not Jews, and because no commandment is given, that therefore we may do less than the Jews. Far be this from him who knows the power of the precious blood of Christ!

My advice is this: if the reader has as yet but little knowledge and little grace, let him accordingly begin with a small percentage, yea, though it were ever so small a percentage, only let him be true to God, and put aside for Him habitually as He may be pleased to prosper him. In this way blessing for the soul will be reaped, will be abundantly reaped, and soon will the desire spring up in the heart to increase the proportion of returns to the Lord. This way will more and more lead the heart to such a state to be only a steward for the Lord, and to be willing to stand with all we have and are before the Lord as His stewards.

The great business of the disciple of the Lord Jesus

This extract is from the third part of Müller's *Narratives*, first published in 1845.

I desire to make a few remarks on Matthew 6:33: 'Seek first the kingdom of God and His righteousness; and all these things shall be added unto you'.

After our Lord, in the previous verses, had been pointing His disciples to the 'fowls of the air' and the 'lilies of the field' in order that they should be without carefulness about the necessities of life, He adds: 'Therefore take no thought, (literally be not anxious) saying, What shall we drink? or, Wherewithal shall we be clothed? (For after all these things do the Gentiles seek); for your Heavenly Father knows that you need all these things.'

Observe here particularly that we, the children of God, should be different from the nations of the earth, from those who have no Father in Heaven, and who therefore make it their great business, their first anxious concern, what they shall eat, and what they shall drink, and how they shall be clothed. We, the children of God, should as in every other respect, so in this particular also, be different from the world, and prove to the world that we believe that we have a Father in Heaven, Who knows that we need all these things.

The fact that our Almighty Father, Who is full of infinite

love to us His children, knows that we need these things should remove all anxiety from our minds.

There is however one thing that we have to attend to, and which we *ought* to attend to, with reference to our temporal necessities, it is mentioned in our verse: 'Seek first the kingdom of God and His righteousness.' The great business which the disciple of the Lord Jesus has to be concerned about (for this word was spoken to disciples, to professed believers) is to seek the kingdom of God, that is to seek, as I view it, after the external and internal prosperity of the Church of Christ.

If, according to our ability, and according to the opportunity which the Lord gives us, we seek to win souls for the Lord Jesus, that appears to me to be seeking the *external prosperity* of the kingdom of God; and if we, as members of the body of Christ, seek to benefit our fellow members in the body, helping them on in grace and truth, or caring for them in any way to their edification, that would be seeking the *internal prosperity* of the kingdom of God.

But in connexion with this we have also 'to seek His righteousness', which means (as it was spoken to disciples, to those who have a Father in Heaven, and not to those who were without) to seek to be more and more like God, to seek to be inwardly conformed to the mind of God.

If these two things are attended to (and *they imply also that we are not slothful in business*), then do we come under that precious promise: 'And all these things [that is food, clothing, or anything else that is needful for this present life], shall be added unto you.' It is not *for* attending to these things that we obtain the blessing, but *in* attending to them.

I now ask you, my dear reader, a few questions in all love, because I do seek your welfare, and I do not wish to put these questions to you without putting them first to my own heart.

Do you make it your primary business, your first great concern, to seek the kingdom of God and His righteousness?

Are the things of God, the honour of His name, the welfare of His Church, the conversion of sinners, and the profit of your own soul, your chief aim?

Or does your business, or your family, or your own temporal concerns, in some shape or other *primarily* occupy your attention?

If the latter be the case, then, though you may have all the necessities of life, yet could you be surprised if you had them not? Remember that the world passes away, but that the things of God endure for ever.

I never knew a child of God who acted according to the above passage, in whose experience the Lord did not fulfil His word of promise, 'All these things shall be added unto you.'

To those engaged in Christian work

Did Müller recommend that all Christian work should be financed in the manner which he found to be so successful for well over sixty years? His answer began with a fundamental point:

Though every believer is not called upon to establish orphan-houses, charity schools, and so on, and trust in the Lord for means (for such a work an especial call is needed), yet all believers are called upon, in the simple confidence of faith, to cast all their burdens upon Him, to trust in Him for everything, and not only to make everything a subject of prayer, but to expect answers to their petitions which they have asked according to His will, and in the name of the Lord Jesus.

But those who have responded to God's call to costly Christian endeavours, or who are contemplating such work for Him, should note these words of Müller written in 1886.

Were the real blessedness of this way *known*, how we carry on the work of God by depending on Him *alone* for help regarding everything, tens of thousands of our dear fellow-labourers, in their work for the Lord, would act on precisely the same principles also.

In the same year Müller listed four conditions which need to be met if God is to sustain Christian enterprises financed according to the faith principle.

First, we have to be sure that the work in which we are engaged is really the *work of the Lord*, and *fully* so. I lay stress on this because I have seen how, in order to keep persons from certain evil things, there have been substituted other evil things, which, though in the sight of some they be less objectionable, yet are of such a character as that they are unworthy of the name of God's work. How then could help be expected from God under such circumstances?

Second, we have to ascertain that *we* are the persons to be engaged in that work which is *really* God's work; for we are not our own, but we are bought with a price, the precious blood of the Lord Jesus. We therefore may not spend our time, our talents, our bodily, mental and spiritual strength as we please; but we have to seek to know whether the Lord would have us to be engaged in such and such a way or not.

Third, we have to seek to ascertain, by patient waiting upon God, watching His hand, whether *His time* is come, that we should do this His work.

How important these last two points are we have clearly shown to us in the building of the temple. The work was a good work, and quite according to the mind of Jehovah; but His time was not yet come that this work was to be done, when David desired to build the temple; nor was he to be the man to do it, but his son Solomon.

Fourth, we have to trust in Him for *all* the help we need. If we do not do so, how could we expect to go on well?

Here I state that the pecuniary necessities for which we have to wait upon the Lord, great though they are, amounting to about forty-four thousand pounds yearly, are very far from all we need. We have constantly to look to the Lord for counsel and guidance in our difficulties; and but for His constant guidance we should make only mistakes and take wrong steps.

What these difficulties were are described on pages 28–29 above.

Living by faith for your personal income

In the fourth part of his *Narratives* Müller set out the conditions which he thought needed to be met by anyone living by faith for his (or her) personal income.

If anyone desires to go this way he must –

Not *merely say* that he trusts in God, but must *really do so*. Often individuals profess to trust in God, but they embrace every opportunity, directly or indirectly, to expose their need and thus to seek to induce persons to help them. I do not say it is wrong to make known our wants; but I do say it ill agrees with trust in God to expose our wants for the sake of inducing persons to help us. God will take us at our word. If we say we trust in Him, He will try whether we *really* do so, or only *profess* to do so; and if *indeed* we trust in Him, we are satisfied to stand with Him alone.

Be willing to be rich or poor, as the Lord pleases. He must be willing to know what it is to have an abundance or scarcely anything. He must be willing to leave this world without any possessions.

Be willing to take the money in God's way, not merely in large sums but in small. Again and again have I had a single shilling given or sent to me. To have refused such tokens of Christian love would have been ungracious.

Be willing to live as the Lord's steward. If anyone were to begin this way of living, and did not communicate out of that which the Lord gives to him, but hoard it up; or, if he would live up to his income, as it is called, then the Lord, who influences the hearts of His children to help him with means, would soon cause those channels to be dried up.

Work and pray

This is how, in 1856, Müller expressed the balance which Christians should achieve between work and prayer.

The disciples of the Lord Jesus should labour with all their might in the work of God as if everything depended on their exertions; and yet, having done so, they should not in the least trust in their labour and efforts, and in the means which they use for the spread of the truth, but in God; and they should with all earnestness seek the blessing of God, in persevering, patient, and believing prayer.

Here is the great secret of success, my Christian reader. Work with all your might; but trust not in the least in your work. Pray with all your might for the blessing of God; but work, at the same time, with all diligence, with all patience, with all perseverance. Pray then, and work. Work and pray. And still again pray, and then work. And so on all the days of your life. The result will surely be abundant blessing. Whether you *see* much fruit or little fruit; *such* kind of service will be blessed.

We should labour then, for instance, with all earnestness in seeking to circulate thousands of copies of the Holy Scriptures, and hundreds of thousands of tracts, as if everything depended upon the amount of copies we circulate; and yet, in reality, we should not in the least degree put our dependence upon the number of copies of the Holy Scriptures, and upon the number of tracts, but entirely upon God for His blessing, without which all these efforts are entirely useless. This blessing however should be sought by us *habitually* and *perseveringly* in prayer. It should also be fully *expected*.

Enjoying God

Müller began a New Year's address at Bethesda Chapel in 1876 by making a characteristic point.

We have through the Lord's goodness been permitted to enter upon another year, and the minds of many amongst us will no doubt be occupied with plans for the future, and the various spheres of service in which, if our lives are spared, we shall be engaged. The welfare of our families, the prosperity of our business, our work and service for the Lord, may be considered the most important matters to be attended to; but, according to my judgment, the most important point to be attended to is this: *above all things, see to it that your souls are happy in the Lord.*

Other things may press upon you; the Lord's work even may have urgent claims upon your attention; but I deliberately repeat, it is of supreme and paramount importance that you should seek above all things to have your souls truly happy in God Himself. Day by day seek to make this the most important business of your life. This has been my firm and settled conviction for the last five and thirty years. For the first four years after my conversion I knew not its vast importance; but now, after much experience, I specially commend this point to the notice of my younger brethren and sisters in Christ. The secret of all true effectual service is – joy in God, and having experimental acquaintance and fellowship with God Himself.

But in what way shall we attain to this settled happiness of soul? How shall we learn to enjoy God? How obtain such an all-sufficient, soul-satisfying portion in Him as shall enable us to let go the things of the world as vain and worthless in comparison? I answer: this happiness is to be obtained through the study of the Holy Scriptures. God has therein revealed Himself unto us in the face of Jesus Christ. In the Scriptures, by the power of the Holy Spirit, He makes Himself known unto our souls.

Müller's hints on how to read the Bible are given on pages 64–71 above.

On reality

During the course of the same address Müller said:

Our holy faith does not consist in *talking*. 'Reality, reality, reality,' is what we want. Let us have *heart-work*; let us be genuine. Brethren and sisters, we should live so as to be missed – missed both in the Church and in the world, when we are removed! Oh how rapidly is time hastening on! We should live in such a manner as that, if we are called hence, our dear brethren and sisters might feel our loss, and from their inmost souls exclaim, 'Oh that such a one were in our midst again!' We ought to be missed even by the world. Worldly persons should be constrained to say of us, 'If ever there was a Christian upon earth, that man was one.'

Epilogue

Epilogue

'The living God is with us, Whose power never fails, Whose arm never grows weary, Whose wisdom is infinite, and Whose power is unchanging. Therefore today, tomorrow, and next month, as long as life is continued, He will be our helper and friend. Still more, even as He is through all time, so will He be through all eternity.'

Müller's successors in Bristol have found that those words their founder wrote are true – at least as far as time is concerned (they cannot yet speak for eternity). They have discovered that God remains, even in the closing decades of the twentieth century, a living reality. No appeals for funds are made and the Directors of The Müller Homes for Children look to this same God to supply their needs.

But while there has been no departure from the principle of reliance on prayer and faith, the *work* of the Homes has changed. In this century the Directors have adapted to new ideas about how children should be cared for, and changing social conditions which have meant that children need care for different reasons.

The great buildings on Ashley Down have been sold and are now the headquarters of Brunel Technical College. The children are looked after by house parents in more luxurious small family group homes, and attend local schools.

The demand for the type of residential care where children 'live in' is much reduced. The official policy today is for needy children to be fostered with individual families wherever possible.

Today there are different problems – which sadly are all too familiar to us. Family units are less secure or may not exist at all. So the Homes are opening Day Care and Family Care Centres to try to help not only children who are in need but also their parents. Professional help and care is offered in a Christian setting.

With far more old people in England than ever before, the

Directors are also hoping to establish The Müller Homes for the Elderly.

Gifts are still sent to missionaries in many parts of the world, amounting currently to about fifty thousand pounds a year.

The tradition established in 1849 when Müller opened his first Bible warehouse is continued in the shape of three busy bookshops – called *Evangelical Christian Literature* – run by the Homes in Bristol, Bath and Weston-Super-Mare. In May, 1984, the Bristol shop set up an out-post at Ashton Gate Football Stadium and was visited by thousands of people who came to hear Billy Graham preach the same gospel which Müller had proclaimed a century earlier.

Since 1958, Müller's mantle has been worn by Mr J. J. Rose who has been ably assisted in recent years by his associate director and social worker Mr J. Cowan. Let us give Jack Rose the final word. In a recent Annual Report of the work of the Homes, he wrote:

'God is immutable. As He was in our yesterday, He is in our today and will be in our tomorrow, hence He knows the end from the beginning. Depending on these truths we launch out in faith. We can observe in the past the way the Lord dealt with George Müller, we can experience Him in our today and be assured that what He has promised of our tomorrow will be perfectly and completely fulfilled. The Scripture says, "Acquaint now yourself with Him and be at peace; because the eternal God is your refuge, and underneath are the everlasting arms."'

Appendix

Partnership with God

This is an extract from the third part of Müller's *Narratives*.

I desire to throw out a few hints on 1 John 1:3: 'And our fellowship is with the Father and with His Son, Jesus Christ.' Observe:

1. The words 'fellowship', 'communion', 'co-participation', and 'partnership' mean the same.

2. The believer in the Lord Jesus does not only obtain forgiveness of all his sins (as he does through the shedding of the blood of Jesus by faith in His name); does not only become a righteous one before God (through the righteousness of the Lord Jesus, by faith in His name); is not only begotten again, born of God, and partaker of the divine nature, and therefore a child of God, and an heir of God; but he is also in fellowship or partnership with God.

Now, so far as it regards God, and our standing in the Lord Jesus, we have this blessing once and for all; nor does it allow of either an increase or a decrease. Just as God's love to us believers, His children, is unalterably the same (whatever may be the manifestations of that love); and as His peace with us is the same, (however much our peace may be disturbed); so it is also with regard to our being in fellowship or partnership with Him: it remains unalterably the same, so far as God is concerned.

3. But then, there is an *experimental* fellowship, or partnership, with the Father and with His Son, which consists in this, that all which we possess in God, as being the partners or fellows of God, is brought down into our daily life, is enjoyed, experienced, and used. This *experimental* fellowship, or partnership, allows of an increase or a decrease, in the measure in which faith is in exercise, and in which we are entering into what we have received in the Lord Jesus. The measure in which we enjoy this *experimental* fellowship with the Father and with the Son is without limit; for without

limit we may make use of our partnership with the Father and with the Son, and draw by prayer and faith out of the inexhaustible fulness which there is in God.

Let us now take a few instances in order to see the practical working of this *experimental* fellowship (or partnership) with the Father, and with the Son.

Suppose there are two believing parents who were not brought to the knowledge of the truth until some years after the Lord had given them several children. Their children were brought up in sinful, evil ways, whilst the parents did not know the Lord. Now the parents reap as they sowed. They suffer from having set an evil example before their children; for their children are unruly and behave most improperly. What is now to be done? Need such parents despair?

No. The first thing they have to do is to make confession of their sins to God with regard to neglecting their children whilst they were themselves living in sin, and then to remember that they are in partnership with God, and therefore to be of good courage, though they are in themselves still utterly insufficient for the task of managing their children. They have in themselves neither the wisdom, nor the patience, nor the long-suffering, nor the gentleness, nor the meekness, nor the love, nor the decision and firmness, nor anything else that may be needful in dealing with their children aright. But their Heavenly Father has all this. The Lord Jesus possesses all this. And they are in partnership with the Father, and with the Son, and therefore they can obtain by prayer and faith all they need out of the fulness of God.

I say by *prayer* and *faith*; for we have to make known our need to God in prayer, ask His help, and then we have *to believe* that He will give us what we need. Prayer alone is not enough. We may pray never so much, yet if we do not believe that God will give us what we need, we have no reason to expect that we shall receive what we have asked for.

So then these parents would need to ask God to give them the needful wisdom, patience, long-suffering, gentleness, meekness, love, decision, firmness, and whatever else they may judge they need. They may in humble boldness remind their Heavenly Father that His word assures them that they are in partnership with Him, and, as they themselves are lacking in these particulars, ask Him to be pleased to supply their need; and then they have *to believe* that God will do it, and they shall receive according to their need.

Another instance: suppose I am so situated in my business that day by day such difficulties arise that I continually find that I take wrong steps by reason of these great difficulties. How may the case be altered for the better? In myself I see no remedy for the difficulties. In looking at myself I can expect nothing but to make still further mistakes, and therefore trial upon trial seems to be before me. And yet I need not despair. The living God is my partner. *I* have not sufficient wisdom to meet these difficulties so as to be able to know what steps to take, but *He* is able to direct me.

What I have therefore to do is this: in simplicity to spread my case before my Heavenly Father and my Lord Jesus. The Father and the Son are my partners. I have to tell out my heart to God, and to ask Him that, as He is my partner, and I have no wisdom in myself to meet all the many difficulties which continually occur in my business, He would be pleased to guide and direct me, and to supply me with the needful wisdom; and then I have *to believe* that God will do so, and go with good courage to my business, and *expect* help from Him in the next difficulty that may come before me. *I have to look out* for guidance, *I have to expect* counsel from the Lord; and, as assuredly as I do so, I shall have it, I shall find that I am not nominally but really in partnership with the Father and with the Son.

Another instance: there are a father and a mother with seven small children. Both parents are believers. The father works in a manufactory, but cannot earn more than ten shillings per week. The mother cannot earn anything. These ten shillings are too little for the supply of nourishing and wholesome food for seven growing children and their parents, and for providing them with the other necessities of life.

What is to be done in such a case? Surely not to find fault with the manufacturer, who may not be able to afford more wages, and much less to murmur against God; but the parents have in simplicity to tell God, their partner, that the wages of ten shillings a week are not sufficient in England to provide nine persons with all they need so as that their health be not injured.

They have to remind God that He is not a hard master, not an unkind Being, but a most loving Father, who has abundantly proved the love of His heart in the gift of His only begotten Son. And they have in childlike simplicity to ask Him that either He would order it so that the manufacturer may be able to allow more wages; or that He (the Lord) would find them another place, where the father would be able to earn more; or that He would be pleased somehow or other, as it may seem good to Him, to supply them with more means.

They have to ask the Lord, in childlike simplicity, again and again for it if He does not answer their request at once; and they have *to believe* that God, their Father and partner, will give them the desire of their hearts. They have *to expect* an answer to their prayers; day by day they have *to look out* for it, and to repeat their request till God grants it. As assuredly as they *believe* that God will grant them their request, so assuredly it shall be granted.

Thus suppose I desired more power over my besetting sins; suppose I desired more power against certain temptations; suppose I desired more wisdom, or grace, or anything else that I may need in my service among the saints, or in my service towards the unconverted: what have I to do, but to make use of my being in fellowship with the Father and with the Son?

Just as for instance an old faithful clerk, who is this day taken into partnership by an immensely rich firm, though himself altogether without property, would not be discouraged by reason of a large payment having to be made by the firm within three days, though he himself has no money at all of his own, but would comfort himself with the immense riches possessed by those who so generously have just taken him into partnership: so should we, the children of God and servants of Jesus Christ, comfort ourselves by being in fellowship, or partnership, with the Father and with the Son, though we have no power of our own against our besetting sins; though we cannot withstand temptations which are before us in our own strength; and though we have neither sufficient grace nor wisdom for our service among the saints, or towards the unconverted. All we have to do is to draw upon our partner, the living God.

But *if we do not believe* that God will help us, could we be at peace? The clerk, taken into the firm as partner, *believes* that the firm will meet the payment though so large, and though in three days it is to be made, and it is this that keeps his heart quiet, though altogether poor himself. We have to believe that our infinitely rich partner, the living God, will help us in our need, and we shall not only be in peace, but we shall actually find that the help which we need will be granted to us.

Let not the consciousness of your entire unworthiness keep you, dear reader, from believing what God has said concerning you. If you are indeed a believer in the Lord Jesus, then this precious privilege of being in partnership with the Father and the Son is yours, though you and I are entirely unworthy of it. If the consciousness of our unworthiness were to keep us from believing what God has said concerning those who depend upon and trust in the Lord Jesus for salvation, then we should find that there is not one single blessing with which we have been blessed in the Lord Jesus, from which, on account of our unworthiness, we could derive any settled comfort or peace.

Main events of Müller's life

1805 (September 27)	Born, Kroppenstedt, Prussia.
1810	The family move to Heimersleben. His father is appointed collector of taxes.
1820	His mother dies.
1821	Arrested for debt in Wolfenbüttel. Spends four weeks in prison.
1825 (Easter)	Enters Halle University to study theology under Friedrich Tholuck.
1825 (November)	Becomes a Christian following a visit to a small house meeting.
1828 (March)	Graduates at Halle.
1829 (January)	Rejected from army service on grounds of 'a tendency to tuberculosis'.

1829 (March)	Arrives in London to train with the London Society for Promoting Christianity among the Jews (now the Church Mission to the Jews).
1829 (May)	Falls ill. Believes he is dying.
1829 (Summer)	Convalescence in Teignmouth, Devon. Meets Henry Craik and becomes associated with founders of Brethren movement.
1830 (January)	Ends association with London Society for Promoting Christianity among the Jews.
1830	Becomes pastor of Ebenezer Chapel in Teignmouth.
1830 (August)	Marries Mary Groves (sister of Anthony Norris Groves) in Exeter.
1830 (October)	Pew-rents abandoned at Ebenezer Chapel. Müller gives up a regular salary.
1832 (May)	Müller and Henry Craik accept an invitation to become pastors of Gideon Chapel in Bristol.
1832 (June)	Müller and Craik begin to work at Bethesda Chapel, Bristol.
1834	Establishes Scriptural Knowledge Institution for Home and Abroad.
1836 (April)	Opens first children's home in Wilson Street, Bristol, for thirty children. Subsequently opens three further homes in same street.
1837 (June)	Princess Victoria becomes Queen.
1841	His father dies.
1848	Split between 'Open' and 'Exclusive' Brethren (followers of J. N. Darby).
1849 (June)	Opens new purpose-built home on Ashley Down, Bristol, for three hundred children (now Allen House).
1857	Second Ashley Down home open (Brunel House).

1862	Third Ashley Down home open (subsequently named Müller House).
1866 (January)	Henry Craik dies.
1866	Dr Barnardo opens children's home in London.
1869	Fourth Ashley Down home open (Davy House).
1870	Final Ashley Down home open (Cabot House). Now cares for two thousand children and employs over two hundred staff.
1870 (February)	Mary Müller dies.
1870s	Sends £10,000 abroad annually to nearly two hundred missionaries.
1871 (November)	Marries Susannah Sangar.
1875	Begins preaching tours. Travels two hundred thousand miles to forty-two countries.
1878 (January)	Meets President of United States and (with Susannah) is conducted around the White House.
1881	Church of England Children's Society opens first home.
1892 (May)	Last preaching tour ends.
1894 (January)	Susannah Müller dies.
1895 (September)	Ninetieth birthday presentation at Bethesda Chapel.
1897 (June)	Preaches at Bethesda Chapel on occasion of Queen Victoria's Diamond Jubilee.
1898 (March 9)	Leads evening prayer meeting on Ashley Down.
1898 (March 10)	Dies peacefully at 6.00 a.m., aged ninety-two.

Current address of Müller's Homes:
The Müller Homes for Children
Müller House
7 Cotham Park
Bristol BS6 6DA